THE ROYAL COURT THEATRE PRESENTS

Pah-La

by Abhishek Majumdar

Pah-La was developed with the support of Re-imagine India, Arts Council England. The playwright was supported by a grant from the Foundation for Universal Responsibility of HH The Dalai Lama.

Pah-La was first performed at the Royal Court Jerwood Theatre Upstairs, Sloane Square, on Wednesday 3 April 2019.

Pah-La

by Abhishek Majumdar

CAST (in alphabetical order)

Constable Gaphel **Paul Chan**
Dorjee/Jia **Tuyen Do**
Pema **Zachary Hing**
Rinpoche/Man with a Stick **Kwong Loke**
Tsering **Richard Rees**
Ling **Gabby Wong**
Deshar/Liu **Millicent Wong**
Deng **Daniel York Loh**

Director **Debbie Hannan**
Designer **Lily Arnold**
Lighting Designer **Jessica Hung Han Yun**
Composer & Sound Designer **Tom Gibbons**
Movement Director **Quang Kien Van**
Casting Director **Amy Ball**
Production Manager **Marty Moore**
Costume Supervisor **Sydney Florence**
Assistant Director **Abigail Sewell**
Associate Sound Designer **Ben Grant**
Additional music by **Tashi Monlam, Anonymous**
Costume Assistants **Imogen Brown, Grace Drake, Amy Yeates**
Stage Managers **Fiona Kennedy, Andy McCarthy**
Stage Management Work Placement **Amy Grudniewicz**
Set built by **Richard Nutbourne Scenic Studio**

Special thanks to:
Darig K. Thokmay & Tenzing Zega

Pah-La
by Abhishek Majumdar

Abhishek Majumdar (Writer)

As writer, for the Royal Court: **The Djinns of Eidgah (& Writers' Bloc Festival, Mumbai/Hindu MetroPlus Theatre Festival, Bangalore/Hamilton Fringe Festival, Ontario); The Ocean [short audio play on Climate Change].**

As writer, other theatre includes: **Pratidwandi [adaptation] (& Dharwad Theatre Festival), Lucknow '76 (& Alliance Francaise, Bangalore), Harlesden High Street (& Tara Arts), An Arrangement of Shoes (& Cock Tavern/ Theatre503/Edinburgh Festival Fringe/Exeter Fringe Festival/Acoustic Arts Festival), Niharika, Dweepa (Ranga Shankara, Bangalore); Land of Ups & Downs (Headstart Academy, Bangalore); Linea Historica/The Prophet (Festival Internacionale de Dramaturgia, Buenos Aires); 399 (Climate Change Theatre Action).**

As director, other theatre includes: **Waterlines [adaptation] (National Gallery of Modern Art, Bangalore); Gasha (Prithvi, Mumbai/ Ranga Shankara/Tour); Thook (Deutsch Schauspielhaus, Hamburg/Ranga Shankara/ Goethe Institut, Bangalore/Carriage House, Hartford/Yale); Treadmill (Ranga Shankara/ Jagriti, Bangalore/Prithvi/Tour); #supernova (Deutsch Schauspielhaus, Freiburg/Goethe Institut/Theater Freiburg); Tathagat (Jan Natya Manch, Delhi); Eidgah ke Jinnat (Jawahar Kala Kendra, Jaipur).**

As writer & director, other theatre includes: **Rizwaan (FTII Pune/Ranga Shankara); Kaumudi, Afterlife of Birds, Muktidham (Ranga Shankara/Prithvi/ Tour).**

Awards include: **Hindu Metroplus Playwright's Award (Harlesden High Street); Mahindra Excellence in Theatre Awards for Best Play & Best Ensemble (Gasha); Mahindra Excellence in Theatre Award for Best Original Script (Muktidham); Toto Funds the Arts Writer's Award; International Centre for Women Playwrights 50/50 Applause Award.**

Abhishek attended the 2011 Royal Court International Residency for Emerging Playwrights. He was given the Shankar Nag Rangakarmi Theatre Award (given to artists under 35) for a decade's contribution to Theatre in India.

Lily Arnold (Designer)

Theatre includes: **The Remains of the Day, Rules for Living (Royal & Derngate, Northampton); Sleeping Beauty (Theatre Royal, Stratford East); The Unreturning [costume] (Frantic Assembly); Things of Dry Hours, The Scottsboro Boys (Young Vic); Snow in Midsummer, The Jew of Malta,** The Rape of Lucrece, King Lear, The Taming of the Shrew (RSC); Room (Abbey, Dublin/Theatre Royal, Stratford East); Love Lies Bleeding (Print Room); Henry V (Tobacco Factory); The Secret Garden (Theatre by the Lake); The Girl on the Train, The Fruit Trilogy, Blake Remixed (Leeds Playhouse); Dublin Carol (Sherman); Broken Biscuits (Paines Plough/Live); Bits of Me Are Falling Apart (Soho); The Solid Life of Sugar Water (National/Theatre Royal, Plymouth); The Sugar Coated Bullets of the Bourgeoisie (HighTide/Arcola); Tomcat (Southwark); Jeramee, Hartleby & Ooglemore (Unicorn); Forget Me Not (Bush); So Here We Are (HighTide, Royal Exchange, Manchester); Gruesome Playground Injuries, The Edge of Our Bodies (Gate); Beached (Marlowe, Canterbury); Up & Out Christmas Sprout (Northern Stage); Yellow Face (Park/NT Shed); Peddling (HighTide/59E59, NYC); Things Will Never Be the Same Again (Kiln); Happy New (West End); Ahasverus, The Bullet (Hampstead); A Season in the Congo (Young Vic).

Opera includes: **Opera Scenes (National Opera Studio).**

Paul Chan (Constable Gaphel)

Theatre includes: **The Fu Manchu Complex (Ovalhouse/Moongate); The Best Man (Yellow Earth); Robin Hood, Oliver Twist! (Blah Blah Blah); Typhoon I-V (East Asian Playreading Festival/Yellow Earth); East West United (Soho); Bus Stop (Royal Exchange, Manchester); The Big Magic (Polka); Romeo & Juliet (Basingstoke Haymarket); Frying Circus, Takeaway (Mu-Lan); Hamlet (Singapore Rep).**

Television includes: **Action Team, Benidorm, Trolled, Doctors, Hank Zipzer, The Tracey Ullman Show, Pompidou, Cockroaches, Stella, The Morgana Show, Johnny Shakespeare, Green Wing, Sweet & Sour Comedy, The Missing Chink, Chinese Philosophy for Beginners, Mersey Beat, Emmerdale, Crimewatch UK.**

Film includes: **Blue Iguana, Finding Your Feet, Lucy, Brash Young Turks, As You Like It, Same Same But Different, Offending Angels, Everybody Loves Sunshine.**

Radio includes: **Death at the Airport: The Plot Against Kim Jong-Nam, Inspector Chen - The Mao Case, The Good Listener, Victory, The View from Here: Demolition Man, Bare Branches, One Day in the Life of Ivan Denisovich, Monkey, Waiting for the Earth to Move.**

Tuyen Do (Dorjee/Jia)

Theatre includes: **The Great Wave (National); Mothergun (West End); Mothers & Daughters [scratch], Unbroken (Tamasha); Golden Child (New Diorama); A Dream from a Bombshell, The Grammar of Love (Ovalhouse).**

Television includes: **EastEnders, Different for Girls, 24: Live Another Day, Scrutiny, My So Called Life Sentence.**

Film includes: **The Trip, Healthy, Cross Your Fingers, Happy Accident, Interval, My Dad the Communist [short]; The Ones Below, Luck.**

Sydney Florence
(Costume Supervisor)

For the Royal Court: **Wig Out [as assistant], Wanderlust, Disconnect.**

Other theatre includes: **Love's Labour's Lost, Lions & Tigers, All's Well That Ends Well, All the Angels, The Merchant of Venice, Two Gentlemen of Verona, The Comedy of Errors, Much Ado About Nothing, Holy Warriors, The Taming of the Shrew, Much Ado About Nothing (Globe); Frozen, Witness for the Prosecution (West End); A Tale of Two Cities (Regents Park Open Air); They Drink It In the Congo, Ruined, Chain Play (Almeida); Shakespeare in Love, Abigails Party (Theatre Royal, Bath); The Mentor, Half Life, Forever Yours Mary Lou, Monsieur Popular (Ustinov, Bath); Sleeping Beauty, Room, The Bubbly Black Girl Loses Her Chameleon Skin (Theatre Royal, Stratford East); Approaching Empty, The Bomb, Stones in His Pockets, Broken Glass, The Great Game: Afghanistan, Women, Power & Politics, Greta Garbo Came to Donegal, Not Black & White season: Cat B, Carpe Diem & Detaining Justice, Radio Golf, Let There be Love, Doubt, Called to Account, Fabulation (Kiln); Baddies, Jeramee Hartleby & Ooglemoore, Snowchild, Edward the Fifth, The Velveteen Rabbit, The Nutcracker (Unicorn); The Secret Garden (Theatre by the Lake); The Nap (Crucible, Sheffield); Absence of War (Headlong); The Country Wife, Mogadishu, The Comedy of Errors (Royal Exchange, Manchester).**

Opera includes: **Agrippina (Grange Park Festival).**

Tom Gibbons
(Composer & Sound Designer)

For the Royal Court: **The Woods, Goats, Love Love Love.**

Other theatre includes: **All About Eve (West End); Hexenjagd (Theater Basel); The Wild Duck (Almeida); The Madness of George III (Nottingham Playhouse); Home, I'm Darling (Theatr Clwyd/National/West End); Oedipus (Toneelgroep, Amsterdam); Hamlet, Oresteia (Almeida/West End); Fanny & Alexander, The Lorax (Old Vic); Hedda Gabler, Sunset at the Villa Thalia, The Red Barn, People Places &**
Things (National/West End); A View From the Bridge (& West End), Life of Galileo, Happy Days, A Season in the Congo, Disco Pigs (Young Vic); Les Misérables (Wermland Opera, Sweden); The Crucible (Broadway); Anna Karenina (Royal Exchange, Manchester); The Moderate Soprano, Elephants (Hampstead); White Devil, As You Like It (RSC); Translations, Plenty (Crucible, Sheffield); Mr Burns, 1984 (Almeida/West End/Broadway); The Absence of War, Romeo & Juliet (Headlong); Lion Boy (Complicité); Henry IV, Julius Caesar (Donmar/St Ann's, Brooklyn); Grounded (Gate); The Spire (Salisbury Playhouse); Roundabout Season (& Shoreditch Town Hall), London, The Angry Brigade, Wasted (Paines Plough); The Rover (Hampton Court Palace); Dead Heavy Fantastic (Liverpool Everyman); Chalet Lines, The Knowledge, Little Platoons, Fifty Ways to Leave Your Lover (Bush).

Awards include: **Olivier Award for Best Sound Design (People, Places & Things).**

Debbie Hannan (Director)

As director, for the Royal Court: **Latir (& Compania Nacional de Mexico), Primetime, Who Cares, Spaghetti Ocean, Peckham: The Soap Opera.**

As assistant director, for the Royal Court: **The Mistress Contract, The Nether, Teh Internet is Serious Business, Birdland, How to Hold Your Breath, God Bless the Child.**

As director, other theatre includes: **Things of Dry Hours (Young Vic); Cuckoo, The Session (Soho); Girl Meets Boy (Yard/National Theatre of Scotland); The Angry Brigade, The Wonderful World of Dissocia (RCS); Pandora (Etch/Pleasance); What We Know, Killer Joe, Conspiracy (RWCMD); Lot & His God, Notes from the Underground (Citizens); liberty, equality, fraternity (Tron/Traverse); PANORAMA (Arches); Woman of the Year (Òran Mór); Nights at the Circus (Paradok).**

As associate director, other theatre includes: **Our Ladies of Perpetual Succour (National Theatre of Scotland/National/West End/International tour); Constellations (West End/UK tour); Little on the Inside (Clean Break).**

As assistant director, other theatre includes: **The Maids, Sleeping Beauty (Citizens); A Pacifist's Guide to the War on Cancer (Complicité/National); Enquirer, A Doll's House (National Theatre of Scotland); Kurt Weill: Double Bill (Scottish Opera).**

As writer, theatre includes: **SHAME: A DOUBLE BILL (Bang Bang Bang Group); Vinyl Idol [co-writer] (Òran Mór).**

Zachary Hing (Pema)

Theatre includes: **Forgotten (Yellow Earth/Moongate); Why is the Sky Blue? (Southwark); Jubilee (Royal Exchange, Manchester/Lyric, Hammersmith); Frantic Ignition (Stratford Circus Arts Centre).**

Jessica Hung Han Yun
(Lighting Designer)

Theatre includes: **The Party's Over (Nonsuch); Becoming Shades (Chivaree Circus); Hive City Legacy (Hot Brown Honey/Roundhouse); Nine Foot Nine (Sleepless/Bunker); One (Bert & Nasi); The Human Voice, Dear Elizabeth (Gate); Forgotten (Yellow Earth/Moongate); Cuckoo (Soho); Snowflake (Old Fire Station); Equus (Theatre Royal, Stratford East/ETT).**

Quang Kien Van (Movement Director)

As choreographer, for the Royal Court: **Goats; Tottenham Symphony, Bunny Dance (Beyond the Court).**

As performer, for the Royal Court: **Teh Internet Is Serious Business.**

As choreographer, other theatre includes: **Boots (Bunker); Forgotten (Yellow Earth/Moongate); Mid-Autumn Dances, Lunar Shadows (QKV Projects); SHAME: Parts One & Two (Bang Bang Bang Group); Lunar Orbits, Lunar Corps (Chinese Arts Space).**

As performer, dance includes: **Miaan, SisGo, Innocence (Scottish Dance); Blake Diptych, Disgo (Darkin Ensemble); View from the Shore (Jacky Lansley Dance); O (Michael Clark Company); Mystere (Cirque du Soleil); Interview, Flying the Rainbow (Oxytoc Dance Project);Tchaikovsky Trilogy, Hamlet, Midnight Express, Romeo & Juliet, Kermesseni Brugge, The King, HC Anderson (Peter Schaufuss Ballet); Othello, XXX CLOSEUP, Where I End & We Begin, Ultimate Ophelia, Loose Ends, Magma (Skanes Dansteater); Matthew Bourne's Swan Lake (Adventures in Motion Pictures).**

As performer, opera includes: **Skin Deep (Opera North); Ariodante (ENO).**

Kwong Loke (Rinpoche/Man with a Stick)

For the Royal Court: **New & Now: Plays from China, You For Me For You, You Never Touched the Dirt (& Edinburgh International Festival).**

Other theatre includes: **The Great Wave (National); Labour of Love (West End); Dear Elizabeth, Tibetan Inroads (Gate); The Luly Plays (Almeida); Hiawatha (Bristol Old Vic); Global Baby Factory (Yellow Earth); Summer Rolls (Rich Mix); The Changeling (Finborough); Rashomon, Scenes from Paradise (Riverside Studios); The Magic Paintbrush, The Snow Lion (Polka); Blue Remembered Hills (UK tour); Two Gentlemen of Verona (Singapore Drama Centre); The Soldier's Tale (Southbank).**

Television includes: **The Feed, Gangs of London, As Time Goes By, Love Hurts, Blue Peter, Casualty, The Knock, The Monkey King.**

Radio includes: **At Sea on Inya Lake, Another Land, Our Father the Mountain, Joy Luck Club.**

Abigail Sewell (Assistant Director)

As director, theatre includes: **Never Forget (Tristan Bates); Heard (Camden People's).**

As assistant director, theatre includes: **Rosenbaum's Rescue (Park); Things of Dry Hours (Young Vic); Random Selfies (Ovalhouse); Timbuktu (Theatre Royal, Stratford East).**

Richard Rees (Tsering)

Theatre includes: **The Jew of Malta, Love's Sacrifice, Volpone, Snow In Midsummer (RSC); The Love Girl & the Innocent (Southwark); #aiww: The Arrest of Ai Weiwei (Hampstead); 66 Books (Bush); Love the Sinner (National); Another Paradise (Kali); Cinderella, Tears of the Indians, Twelfth Night (Nuffield, Southampton); Three Sisters, Queen of Spades & I (Orange Tree); Little Red Riding Hood, Worlds Apart (Theatre Royal, Stratford East); M Butterfly (West End); The Taming of the Shrew, Antony & Cleopatra (Theatr Clwyd/Theatre Royal, Haymarket); A Midsummer Night's Dream, The Merry Wives of Windsor, Twelfth Night, Bashville (Regent's Park Open Air); Measure for Measure (Royal Exchange, Manchester); The White Devil, The Way of the World, The Seagull (Citizens); Under Milk Wood (Worcester).**

Television includes: **Law & Order, Silent Witness, Do Not Be Afraid, Pinochet's Progress, In the Beginning, EastEnders, Crossing the Line, Death on Everest, Bugs, The Healer, Red Eagle.**

Film includes: **Vacant Possession, The Omen, Aberdeen, Darklands, On Dangerous Ground.**

Gabby Wong (Ling)

Theatre includes: **Dear Elizabeth (Gate); ManColn (VAULT Festival); Troilus & Cressida, The Jew of Malta, Love's Sacrifice, Volpone (RSC); The Winter's Tale, Macbeth (National); Doctor Faustus (West End); Takeaway, Sinbad the Sailor (Theatre Royal, Stratford East); Posh (Pleasance); Brave New World (Creation); Last Days of Limehouse (Yellow Earth); Beat My Time Machine Skipped (Soho); Venus Flytrap, Numbers of Memory (Tamasha); Othello (Globe).**

Television includes: **Strangers.**

Film includes: **Rogue One: A Star Wars Story, Random 11, Aliceville, Simana.**

Radio includes: **Avenue of Eternal Peace, One of Two Stories or Both, The Man Who Tended Dahlias.**

Millicent Wong (Deshar/Liu)

Theatre includes: **Forbidden City: Portrait of an Empress (Singapore Rep); Beauty World (Dick Lee Entertainment); Hanuman (Imitating the Dog).**

Pah-La is Millicent's UK theatre debut.

Daniel York Loh (Deng)

For the Royal Court: **New & Now: Plays from China, Porcelain.**

Other theatre includes: **The Merchant of Venice, The Country Wife, Moby Dick, Snow In Midsummer, Dido Queen of Carthage (RSC); Welcome Home Captain Fox! (Donmar); The World of Extreme Happiness (National); The Shadow Factory (Nuffield, Southampton); Our American Cousin, We Know Where You Live, P'yongyang (Finborough); Une Tempete (Gate); The Magic Fundoshi (Lyric, Hammersmith); Hamlet (Riverside Studios); Sun Is Shining (King's Head/ BAC/59E59 NYC); The Changeling (Southwark); Branded (Old Vic); Turandot (Hampstead); The Tempest (National/Tour); Measure for Measure (Manchester Library); Nativity (Birmingham Rep); King Lear (Shanghai/UK tour); The Good Woman Of Setzuan (Leicester Haymarket); In the Bag (Traverse); Tartuffe, Romeo & Juliet (Basingstoke Haymarket); Five Tanks (Hackney Empire); Made in England (Contact, Manchester/Birmingham Rep); Blind (Courtyard); The Birds (Aquila, NYC/US tour); The Glass Menagerie, Kiss of the Spider Woman (Singapore Rep); The Importance of Being Earnest, Boeing Boeing (Wild Rice, Singapore); Freud's Last Session (Esplanade, Singapore); Dealer's Choice (Pangdemonium, Singapore); Starring Hitler as Jekyll & Hyde (Finger Players, Singapore).**

As writer, theatre includes: **The Fu Manchu Complex (Ovalhouse/Moongate); Forgotten (Yellow Earth/ Moongate).**

Television includes: **Whitechapel, Moving On, Waking the Dead, Casualty, Peggy Su!, Chambers, The Bill, Supper at Emmaus, A Fish Named Tao, Hollyoaks, Strangers.**

Film includes: **Scarborough, The Receptionist, Rogue Trader, The Beach, Faraway, Act of Grace, Doom.**

Radio includes: **Doggie's Nirvana, Romeo & Juliet, The Monkey King, Dead Lines, Say It with Flowers, Inspector Chen, The Odyssey Project: Telemachus, Death at the Airport.**

Daniel is featured in the best-selling essay collection _The Good Immigrant_.

THE ROYAL COURT THEATRE

The Royal Court Theatre is the writers' theatre. It is a leading force in world theatre for energetically cultivating writers – undiscovered, emerging and established.

Through the writers, the Royal Court is at the forefront of creating restless, alert, provocative theatre about now. We open our doors to the unheard voices and free thinkers that, through their writing, change our way of seeing.

Over 120,000 people visit the Royal Court in Sloane Square, London, each year and many thousands more see our work elsewhere through transfers to the West End and New York, UK and international tours, digital platforms, our residencies across London, and our site-specific work. Through all our work we strive to inspire audiences and influence future writers with radical thinking and provocative discussion.

The Royal Court's extensive development activity encompasses a diverse range of writers and artists and includes an ongoing programme of writers' attachments, readings, workshops and playwriting groups. Twenty years of the International Department's pioneering work around the world means the Royal Court has relationships with writers on every continent.

Within the past sixty years, John Osborne, Samuel Beckett, Arnold Wesker, Ann Jellicoe, Howard Brenton and David Hare have started their careers at the Court.
Many others including Caryl Churchill, Athol Fugard, Mark Ravenhill, Simon Stephens, debbie tucker green, Sarah Kane – and, more recently, Lucy Kirkwood, Nick Payne, Penelope Skinner and Alistair McDowall – have followed.

The Royal Court has produced many iconic plays from Lucy Kirkwood's **The Children** to Jez Butterworth's **Jerusalem** and Martin McDonagh's **Hangmen**.

Royal Court plays from every decade are now performed on stage and taught in classrooms and universities across the globe.

It is because of this commitment to the writer that we believe there is no more important theatre in the world than the Royal Court.

Supported using public funding by
ARTS COUNCIL ENGLAND

INTERNATIONAL PLAYWRIGHTS
AT THE ROYAL COURT THEATRE

Over the last three decades, with the late Elyse Dodgson at the helm, the Royal Court Theatre has led the way in the development and production of new international plays. A creative dialogue now exists with theatre makers from over 70 countries, in over 40 languages. This has grown through facilitating work at grass-roots level, developing exchanges which bring UK writers and directors to work with emerging artists around the world in long-term workshops and residencies internationally and in the UK. Most recently we have been working with artists in Argentina, Chile, China, Cuba, Georgia, India, Iran, Japan, Lebanon, Mexico, Palestine, Peru, Russia, South Africa, Syria, Turkey, Ukraine, Uruguay and Zimbabwe.

Through this programme, the Royal Court Theatre has produced many new international plays since 1997, most recently **Goats** by Liwaa Yazji, **Bad Roads** by Natal'ya Vorozhbit and **B** by Guillermo Calderón in 2017, **I See You** by Mongiwekhaya in 2016 and **Fireworks** by Dalia Taha in 2015.

ABHISHEK MAJUMDAR AND THE ROYAL COURT THEATRE

In 2002 the Royal Court's International Director Elyse Dodgson began a successful decade-long partnership with Rage Productions in Mumbai, running a series of writers groups with generations of Indian playwrights. Plays from these groups went on to form a core part of the programme of the Writers' Bloc Festival at the Prithvi Theatre and on tour across India; several went on to production at the Royal Court.

Abhishek Majumdar took part in the group in 2010 and went on to attend the Royal Court International Residency in London in 2011. Then in 2012, a version of **The Djinns of Eidgah** was produced at the Writers' Bloc Festival in a production directed by Richard Twyman. Abhishek and Richard then went on to work on a new production of the play for the Royal Court, which opened in the Jerwood Theatre Upstairs in 2013.

Since 2015, Abhishek has been developing this major new commission for the Royal Court, in partnership with his Bangalore based company Indian Ensemble. This major new play has emerged through extensive research with the Tibetan community in exile in Dharmashala, workshops in London and development support by the British Council through its Reimagine India fund.

ROYAL

COMING UP AT THE ROYAL COURT

6 - 27 Apr

Dismantle This Room

Created by Milli Bhatia, Ingrid Marvin and Nina Segal

DISMANTLE in association with the Bush Theatre

10 May - 15 Jun

White Pearl

By Anchuli Felicia King

14 May - 1 Jun

salt.

By Selina Thompson

Commissioned by MAYK, Theatre Bristol and Yorkshire Festival.

12 - 15 Jun

The Song Project

Created by Chloe Lamford, Wende, Isobel Waller-Bridge and Imogen Knight

With words by **EV Crowe, Sabrina Mahfouz, Somalia Seaton, Stef Smith and Debris Stevenson**

27 Jun - 10 Aug

the end of history...

By Jack Thorne

4 - 27 Jul

seven methods of killing kylie jenner

By Jasmine Lee-Jones

seven methods of killing kylie jenner is part of the Royal Court's Jerwood New Playwrights programme, supported by Jerwood

royalcourttheatre.com

Sloane Square London, SW1W 8AS
⊖ Sloane Square ⇌ Victoria Station
🐦 royalcourt 📘 royalcourttheatre

Supported using public funding by
ARTS COUNCIL ENGLAND

JERWOOD ARTS

ROYAL COURT SUPPORTERS

The Royal Court is a registered charity and not-for-profit company. We need to raise £1.5 million every year in addition to our core grant from the Arts Council and our ticket income to achieve what we do.

We have significant and longstanding relationships with many generous organisations and individuals who provide vital support. Royal Court supporters enable us to remain the writers' theatre, find stories from everywhere and create theatre for everyone.

We can't do it without you.

PUBLIC FUNDING

Arts Council England, London
British Council

TRUSTS & FOUNDATIONS

The Backstage Trust
The Bryan Adams Charitable Trust
The Austin & Hope Pilkington Trust
The Boshier-Hinton Foundation
Martin Bowley Charitable Trust
The Chapman Charitable Trust
Gerald Chapman Fund
CHK Charities
The City Bridge Trust
The Cleopatra Trust
The Clifford Chance Foundation
Cockayne - Grants for the Arts
The Ernest Cook Trust
The Nöel Coward Foundation
Cowley Charitable Trust
The Eranda Rothschild Foundation
Lady Antonia Fraser for The Pinter Commission
Genesis Foundation
The Golden Bottle Trust
The Haberdashers' Company
The Paul Hamlyn Foundation
Roderick & Elizabeth Jack
Jerwood Arts
The Leche Trust
The Andrew Lloyd Webber Foundation
The London Community Foundation
John Lyon's Charity
Clare McIntyre's Bursary
Old Possum's Practical Trust
The Andrew W. Mellon Foundation
The David & Elaine Potter Foundation
The Richard Radcliffe Charitable Trust
Rose Foundation
Royal Victoria Hall Foundation
The Sackler Trust
The Sobell Foundation
Span Trust
John Thaw Foundation
Unity Theatre Trust
The Wellcome Trust
The Garfield Weston Foundation

CORPORATE SPONSORS

Aqua Financial Solutions Ltd
Cadogan
Colbert
Edwardian Hotels, London
Fever-Tree
Gedye & Sons
Greene King
Kirkland & Ellis International LLP
Kudos
MAC

CORPORATE MEMBERS

Platinum
Lombard Odier

Gold
Weil, Gotshal & Manges LLP

Silver
Auerbach & Steele Opticians
Bloomberg
Kekst CNC
Left Bank Pictures
PATRIZIA
No 8 Partnership
Royal Bank of Canada - Global Asset Management
Sloane Stanley
Tetragon Financial Group

For more information or to become a foundation or business supporter contact: support@royalcourttheatre. com/020 7565 5064.

Supported using public funding by
ARTS COUNCIL ENGLAND

INDIVIDUAL SUPPORTERS

Artistic Director's Circle
Eric Abraham
Carolyn Bennett
Samantha & Richard
  Campbell-Breeden
Cas Donald
Jane Featherstone
Lydia & Manfred Gorvy
Jean & David Grier
Charles Holloway
Jack & Linda Keenan
Mandeep & Sarah Manku
Anatol Orient
NoraLee & Jon Sedmak
Deborah Shaw
  & Stephen Marquardt
Matthew & Sian Westerman
Mahdi Yahya
Anonymous

Writers' Circle
Chris & Alison Cabot
Jordan Cook & John Burbank
Scott M. Delman
Virginia Finegold
Michelle & Jan Hagemeier
Chris Hogbin
Mark Kelly & Margaret
  McDonald Kelly
Nicola Kerr
Emma O'Donoghue
Tracy Phillips
Suzanne Pirret
Theo & Barbara Priovolos
Carol Sellars
Maria Sukkar
Jan & Michael Topham
Maureen & Tony Wheeler
Anonymous

Directors' Circle
Ms Sophia Arnold
Dr Kate Best
Katie Bradford
Piers Butler
Sir Trevor & Lady Chinn
Joachim Fleury
David & Julie Frusher
Julian & Ana Garel-Jones
Louis Greig
David & Claudia Harding
Dr Timothy Hyde
Roderick & Elizabeth Jack
Mrs Joan Kingsley
Victoria Leggett
Emma Marsh
Andrew & Ariana Rodger
Sir Paul & Lady Ruddock
Simon Tuttle
Anonymous

Platinum Members
Simon A Aldridge
Moira Andreae
Nick Archdale
Anthony Burton CBE
Clive & Helena Butler
Gavin & Lesley Casey
Sarah & Philippe Chappatte
Andrea & Anthony Coombs
Clyde Cooper
Victoria Corcoran
Mrs Lara Cross
Andrew & Amanda Cryer
Shane & Catherine Cullinane
Matthew Dean
Sarah Denning
Caroline Diamond
The Drabble Family
Denise & Randolph Dumas
Robyn Durie
Mark & Sarah Evans
Sally & Giles Everist
Celeste Fenichel
Emily Fletcher
The Edwin Fox Foundation
Dominic & Claire Freemantle
Beverley Gee
Nick & Julie Gould
The Richard Grand Foundation
Jill Hackel & Andrzej Zarzycki
Carol Hall
Sam & Caroline Haubold
Mr & Mrs Gordon Holmes
Soyar Hophinson
Damien Hyland
Amanda & Chris Jennings
Ralph Kanter
Jim & Wendy Karp
David P Kaskel
  & Christopher A Teano
Vincent & Amanda Keaveny
Peter & Maria Kellner
Mr & Mrs Pawel Kisielewski
Rosemary Leith
Mark & Sophie Lewisohn
The Maplescombe Trust
Christopher Marek Rencki
Frederic Marguerre
Mrs Janet Martin
Andrew McIver
David & Elizabeth Miles
Jameson & Lauren Miller
Barbara Minto
M.E. Murphy Altschuler
Siobhan Murphy
Peter & Maggie Murray-Smith
Sarah Muscat
Liv Nilssen
Andrea & Hilary Ponti
Greg & Karen Reid
Nick & Annie Reid
Corinne Rooney
William & Hilary Russell
Sally & Anthony Salz

Anita Scott
Bhags Sharma
Dr. Wendy Sigle
Andy Simpkin
Paul & Rita Skinner
Brian Smith
John Soler & Meg Morrison
Kim Taylor-Smith
Mrs Caroline Thomas
The Ulrich Family
Monica B Voldstad
Mr N C Wiggins
Anne-Marie Williams
Sir Robert & Lady Wilson
Anonymous

With thanks to our Friends, Silver and Gold Members whose support we greatly appreciate.

DEVELOPMENT COUNCIL
Piers Butler
Chris Cabot
Cas Donald
Sally Everist
Celeste Fenichel
Virginia Finegold
Tim Hincks
Anatol Orient
Andrew Rodger
Sian Westerman

Our Supporters contribute to all aspects of the Royal Court's work including: productions, commissions, writers' groups, International, Participation and Young Court, creative posts, the Trainee scheme and access initiatives as well as providing in-kind support.

For more information or to become a Supporter please contact: support@royalcourttheatre.com/ 020 7565 5049.

ROYAL

ASSISTED PERFORMANCES

Captioned Performances

Captioned performances are accessible for D/deaf, deafened & hard of hearing people as well as being suitable for people for whom English is not a first language.

In the Jerwood Theatre Downstairs
White Pearl: Wed 22 & 29 May, 5 & 12 Jun, 7.30pm
the end of history...: Wed 10, 17 (plus live speech-to-text post-show talk), 24, 31 Jul & 7 Aug 7.30pm

In the Jerwood Theatre Upstairs
salt.: Fri 31 May, 7.45pm
seven methods of killing kylie jenner: Fri 19 & 26 Jul, 7.45pm

Audio Described Performances

Audio described performances are accessible for blind or partially sighted customers. They are preceded by a touch tour (at 1pm) which allows patrons access to elements of theatre design including set & costume.

In the Jerwood Theatre Downstairs
White Pearl: Sat 8 June, 2.30pm
the end of history...: Sat 3 Aug, 2.30pm

COURT

ROYAL

ASSISTED PERFORMANCES

Performances in a Relaxed Environment

Relaxed Environment performances are suitable for those who may benefit from a more relaxed experience.

During these performances:

_ There will be a relaxed attitude to noise in the auditorium; you are welcome to respond to the show in whatever way feels natural
_ You can enter and exit the auditorium when needed
_ We will help you find the best seats
– House lights remained raised slightly

salt.: Sat 25 May, 7.45pm
White Pearl: Sat 1 Jun, 2.30pm
seven methods of killing kylie jenner: Sat 20 Jul, 3pm
the end of history...: Sat 27 Jul, 2.30pm

If you would like to talk to us about your access requirements please contact our Box Office at (0)20 7565 5000 or **boxoffice@royalcourttheatre.com.** A Royal Court Visual Story is available on our website. We also produce a Story Synopsis & Sensory Synopsis which are available on request.

For more information and to book access tickets online, visit

royalcourttheatre.com/assisted-performances

Sloane Square London, SW1W 8AS ⊖ Sloane Square ⇌ Victoria Station
🐦 royalcourt 📘 royalcourttheatre

COURT

ROYAL

BAR & KITCHEN

The Royal Court's Bar & Kitchen aims to create a welcoming and inspiring environment with a style and ethos that reflects the work we put on stage. Our menu consists of simple, ingredient driven and flavour-focused dishes with an emphasis on freshness and seasonality. This is supported by a carefully curated drinks list notable for its excellent wine selection, craft beers and skilfully prepared coffee. By day a perfect spot for long lunches, meetings or quiet reflection and by night an atmospheric, vibrant meeting space for cast, crew, audiences and the general public.

GENERAL OPENING HOURS
Monday – Friday: 10am – late
Saturday: 12noon – late

Advance booking is suggested at peak times.

For more information, visit
royalcourttheatre.com/bar

HIRES & EVENTS

The Royal Court is available to hire for celebrations, rehearsals, meetings, filming, ceremonies and much more. Our two theatre spaces can be hired for conferences and showcases, and the building is a unique venue for bespoke weddings and receptions.

For more information, visit
royalcourttheatre.com/events

Sloane Square London, SW1W 8AS Sloane Square Victoria Station
 royalcourt royalcourttheatre

COURT

"There are no spaces, no rooms in my opinion, with a greater legacy of fearlessness, truth and clarity than this space."

Simon Stephens, Associate Playwright

The Royal Court invests in the future of the theatre, offering writers the support, time and resources to find their voices and tell their stories, asking the big questions and responding to the issues of the moment.

As a registered charity, the Royal Court needs to raise at least £1.5 million every year in addition to our Arts Council funding and ticket income, to keep seeking out, developing and nurturing new voices. Please join us by donating today.

You can donate online at **royalcourttheatre.com/donate** or via our **donation box in the Bar & Kitchen.**

We can't do it without you.

Support the Court

To find out more about the different ways in which you can be involved please contact support@royalcourttheatre.com/ 020 7565 5049

The English Stage Company at the Royal Court Theatre is a registered charity (No. 231242).

Abhishek Majumdar

PAH-LA

OBERON BOOKS
LONDON

WWW.OBERONBOOKS.COM

First published in 2019 by Oberon Books Ltd
521 Caledonian Road, London N7 9RH
Tel: +44 (0) 20 7607 3637 / Fax: +44 (0) 20 7607 3629
e-mail: info@oberonbooks.com
www.oberonbooks.com

PB ISBN: 9781786827104
E ISBN: 9781786827111

Cover image: Niall McDiarmid

Printed and bound by 4EDGE Limited, Hockley, Essex, UK.
eBook conversion by Lapiz Digital Services, India.

10 9 8 7 6 5 4 3 2 1

In memory of Elyse Dodgson:
We will all continue your work around the world. We promise.
Everything I write will forever be yours.

and

For His Holiness The Dalai Lama, who said:
'Write fearlessly. You know I am not God.'
I know, if there is one, it would have a lot to learn from you.
Thank you for your grace, your love, your blessings,
and for telling me that I should take care of myself.
I cannot believe in a god but I believe I sat next to
the closest possible approximation of the idea.
Thank you, your Holiness.

For Nun Deshar, who may have burnt or died,
we will never know. But who went missing days
before the protests in Lhasa in 2008.
You gave your life and started a revolution.

and

For Rinzin. Who was reportedly starved to death in an
unknown prison in Tibet eventually. When we were friends,
you were 10. You are the bravest person I have ever known.
This world needs to be a better place to deserve you.

For Rai

Your parents went to Tibet. It was not free then.

Yours,
Baba

Acknowledgements

There are several people to be thanked. Many who have been part of this long journey with *Pah-la*.

I begin by thanking, first of all, the many who cannot be named. Several Tibetan and Chinese workers, prisoners, students, teachers, mothers, fathers, monks, nuns, policemen, university professors, laborers, musicians, artists, who cannot be named for purposes of security. Without you this play could not have been made. This play is yours.

Thank you to Aravinda Anantharaman for gifting me Tsudnue's book *Kora*.

Thank you Tenzin Tsundue, a real freedom fighter, a poet, a visionary, a friend and a brother. Thank you Tsundue for everything that you have done, all ideas, thoughts and doors that you have opened. Most of all thank you for your beautiful words and for accompanying them with my scenes from the beginning. Much power to you my friend.

Thank you Lhakpa Lhamphuk, a real champion of the good fight. A wonderful theatre maker and head of Tibet Theatre. Thank you Lhakpa La, for your friendship and brotherhood.

Thank you to Lhasang Tsering, a freedom fighter that the world did not hear of as much as it should have. A true inspiration. A real hero of the Tibetan Struggle.

To the Monks of Kirti Monastery on both sides. To the nuns of Dolma Ling Nunnery. To the current Nuns of two Nunneries in Tibet who cannot be named. My deepest gratitude and respect for the fact that you risked your lives so that the rest of us could hear your stories.

To the office of HH the Dalai Lama. To Rajiv Mehrotra and The Foundation for Universal responsibility of His Holiness the Dalai Lama. To Mahesh Dattani, my teacher who showed me the path this time as well.

To my publishers at Oberon Books.

To members of Hong Kong Police department for vital information on the making and use of Polygraph machines. To the extraordinary hacker talent in Bangalore for getting through Chinese firewalls and chat sites like a breeze.

To the ex-members of the Ne Jhong Sum Deh nunnery in Tibet. To Monk Thinley and Monk Pema for explaining details of Madhyamika and other vital questions in Tibetan Buddhism painstakingly over and over. To Monk Tsultrim of the Bon tradition.

To Dorje Tseten of Students for a Free Tibet.

To Arthur, which I know is not your real name. But I am glad you are safe.

To those Chinese workers of Drapchi and Chushur Prisons who have risked their lives to tell their stories and to save the lives of several Tibetan people.

To the children of the primary school which was attacked in Lhasa and whose name I had in a previous draft and then took out consciously. Thank you for sharing your stories when you were older.

To Pema Thang Guesthouse in Mcleodgang. To Hope café.

To Tibetan Children's Village and Tibetan Transit school, Dharmashala

To members of the Tibetan Government in Exile, Dharmashala.

To Gaphel la for opening several doors in Lhasa.

To the incredible community of guides that has made the Himalayan journey on foot possible over the years.

To Irawati Karnik and Anmol Vellani who are always my first dramaturgs. You form my sense of what I am doing. Anmol, for also being the extraordinary teacher and mentor that he is.

To Arundhati Nag, for providing a question everytime we meet, that becomes the seed for art.

To the Shikhar family for being ours.

To Richard Twyman, for being the friend and collaborator with whom this started. For your friendship and intelligence. To Lucy Morisson for meeting the play. To Debbie Hannan for your friendship and talent. Thank you for directing the first production of this play. Forever indebted.

To the entire cast and crew of *Pah-la* at the Royal Court

Theatre Production. To the wonderful staff of the Royal Court Theatre.

To the actors of Tibet Theatre in Mcleodgang.

To Vicky Featherstone and Lucy Davies, for telling us we can fight and fight with dignity. For standing up for what is right. You are true leaders.

To Jocelyn Clarke, my friend and dramaturg.

To PlayCo New York and Kate Leowald for the workshops on *Pah-la* in New York.

To PEN for standing by the play.

Thanks to Foundation for Liberal Arts and Management (FLAME University), Pune and Ashutosh Potdar for giving me the space to write the first draft of *Pah-la*.

To Delhi University, department of English Literature and Haris Qadeer and Subarno Chaterji for inviting me to the visiting fellowship where *Pah-la* was further shaped.

To the direction and playwriting students in India and at New York University in Abu Dhabi, for asking the most unanswerable questions about plays. To all colleagues in Indian Ensemble and NYU Abu Dhabi, over these years, who have supported this work.

To Tibetan Media friends all over the world for standing by this play in its darkest days.

To Arundhati Ghosh, for standing by thick and thin. Always. You fought relentlessly for this play. Thank you.

To Pankaj Mishra, for being the inspiration that he is.

A big thanks to Priyanka Krishna, who was my first research assistant on this play. Without you we couldn't have started.

To my sister, Didia, who raised me with stories, love and care. Without you I couldn't have started in life.

To Pallavi, my wife. For making possibly the most dangerous journey together. For giving me the home that one can get back to after such journeys. For being my first reader and most astute critic. Thank you.

Characters

TSERING (Male. Early 60s. Tibetan)

DESHAR (Female. Early 20s. Tibetan)

RINPOCHE (Male. Late 60s. Tibetan)

DORJEE (Female. Late 20s. Tibetan)

PEMA (Male. 12. Tibetan)

DENG (Male. Late 40s to Early 50s. Han)

CONSTABLE GAPHEL (Male. Late 60s. Tibetan)

LING (Female. Early 30s. Han)

JIA (Played by actor who plays DORJEE)

MAN WITH A STICK (Played by actor who plays RINPOCHE)

Act 1

A room in a nunnery in eastern Tibet. Two beds, a place to pray and some books. Late evening. It's snowing outside.

DESHAR is wearing a soldier's shirt on top of her robes. DORJEE is wiping blood off DESHAR's face. It is slightly swollen.

DORJEE: You stole it!

DESHAR: I asked for it.

DORJEE: He said no.

DESHAR: He was in the shower.

DORJEE: You asked him while he was in the shower?

DESHAR: Yes. It is our shower.

DORJEE: But he was inside it.

DESHAR: So I asked him from outside!

DORJEE: May I take your clothes please?

DESHAR: Aaah… *(In pain as DORJEE presses too hard.)*

DORJEE: You have a cut.

DESHAR: He hit me.

DORJEE: Deshar. You broke his jaw.

DESHAR: I didn't mean to.

DORJEE: You broke his jaw without meaning to break it?

DESHAR: He said once they expel us all, he will make me sing 'for the motherland', in a soldier's uniform.

1

DORJEE: Deshar, he is a Chinese soldier. You are a buddhist nun.

DESHAR: So I wasn't violent or anything.

DORJEE: DESHAR... YOU STOLE HIS CLOTHES, YOU LEFT HIM STRANDED IN THE COLD IN A COLD TOWEL AND YOU BROKE HIS JAW!!.

DESHAR: Look.

DORJEE: What? *(DESHAR opens her fist which was closed so far.)*

DORJEE: What is it?

DESHAR: inner molar *(Laughs.)*

DORJEE: Inner...what.

DESHAR: Here. touch it *(DORJEE touches it.)*

DORJEE: It's a ...TOOTH!

DESHAR: Inner molar. Third from left. *(Pause.)* Third from inside. *(Laughs.)*

DORJEE: You broke his tooth?

DESHAR: It broke. I merely counted.

DORJEE: Their commander is coming in 2 days to examine the nunnery and here you are breaking their teeth.

DESHAR: They cannot expel me. I did the best in class.

DORJEE: They are not expelling nuns for bad results Deshar! It's not the education board.

DESHAR: Aaah...gentle Dorjee gentle. May the Buddha help you...you are so aggressive for a nun.

DORJEE: *(Unable to contain her laughter but trying to.)* you...you broke his...inner...inner *(Looking at DESHAR.)*

2

DESHAR: Molar. 3rd from inside.

DORJEE *(In disbelief.)* How did you /

DESHAR: His mouth was open.

DORJEE: You hit him with his mouth open? *(Bursts out laughing.)*

DESHAR: I hit his jaw. It dropped, the tooth was dangling, I plucked it.

DORJEE: You plucked his *(Laughs and falls on the floor laughing.)*

DESHAR: I helped him. A hanging tooth is very painful.

DORJEE: There is blood downstairs. In front of Rinpoche's room.

DESHAR: I am the one bleeding *(Shows her small wound.)*

DORJEE: You have a scratch. he has a broken jaw and a missing tooth.

DESHAR: It's my blood.

DORJEE: When Rinpoche finds out.

DESHAR: He isn't going to go to Rinpoche and say that a nun broke his jaw.

DORJEE: He has seen your face. He will have you expelled.

DESHAR: He didn't see my face.

DORJEE: How?

DESHAR: It was covered.

DORJEE *(Bursts out laughing.)* So you knew you were going to hit him!

(Pause.)

Why did you want his clothes?

DESHAR: What did they say at lunch time?

DORJEE: Who?

DESHAR: The soldiers who came in.

DORJEE: They said, their commander will be here in 2 days, in the new train and that they will give us reeducation.

DESHAR: And?

DORJEE: And those nuns who are not needed in the nunnery will be sent away.

DESHAR: And??

DORJEE: What?

DESHAR: This does not make you angry?

DORJEE: I sometimes don't believe you are the top of your class Deshar.

DESHAR: I asked him from outside the shower.

DORJEE: What?

DESHAR: Sir…what are you going to do with me If you take me away *(DORJEE and DESHAR laugh.)*

DORJEE: Why did you do that.

DESHAR: The Buddha is for sarcasm.

DORJEE: Yes… Sarcasm is non violent *(Laughing.)*

DESHAR: But he took it seriously.

DORJEE: Not surprised.

DESHAR: he said *(Pretending to be him.)* " We will parade you in soldier's fatigues and make you sing for the motherland" and then he laughed like a hyena.

DORJEE: Like a what?

DESHAR (Still pretending to be the soldier in the washroom, emulates a horrific laugh which she calls laughing like a hyena.)

DORJEE: Then?

DESHAR: Then I said *(Being herself but overdramatic.)* Sir, then I'll just take your clothes right away and follow the path of liberation *(DORJEE laughs.)*

DESHAR: " If you touch my clothes, I will have you thrown out on the first day the commander arrives" *(Does his laugh again.)*

DORJEE: So you covered your face *(Laughs.)*

DESHAR: I picked up his clothes and showed him from the window. He came running out saying you Tibetan bitch…I will bite your ears off and/

DORJEE: And so you broke his tooth!.

DESHAR: *(Still enacting.)* No, he came out like this and I was standing here with my face covered. I was going away, when he walked out of the shower and kicked me and I, out of sheer reflex, *(In this time, RINPOCHE is at the door. DORJEE has spotted him and is standing with her head down while DESHAR is lost in her story.)*

Landed an elbow to the left of his *(Showing his face.)* and as he fell I plucked his tooth and said *(She enacts plucking his tooth.)* 'My brother, I am sorry you will not bite me. I am sorry brother, you will not bite anyone, anymore'.

(She is laughing as she notices RINPOCHE. Stands up abruptly. Looks at DORJEE. Tries to take the solder's shirt off. Stops. Bows down with folded hands. RINPOCHE looks at her.)

A beat.

(End of scene.)

SCENE 2

TSERING's house. PEMA (12 years old.) is sitting next to him. RINPOCHE and DESHAR are standing. Still Snowing outside.

TSERING: *(To Pema.)* Everything that's circled.

PEMA: Teacher Tsering, but everything is circled! *(Pause.)* I mean /

TSERING: What's your language Pema?

PEMA: Tibetan, Teacher.

TSERING: What kind of Tibetan?

RINPOCHE: May we/

TSERING: I am with a student. You may help yourself to some tea.

RINPOCHE: I am sorry but/

TSERING: It's there. The girl knows.

(BEAT.) YES PEMA. WHAT KIND OF TIBETAN?

PEMA: Our kind Teacher.

TSERING: Everything circled is Mandarin.

PEMA: Teacher…but…this word here/

TSERING: It's used like Mandarin. You cannot use every language the same way Pema. You lose your language,

6

you lose who you are, what you are and most importantly, why... *(Looks at RINPOCHE.)* Why you are. You understand? *(PEMA looks at DESHAR. DESHAR makes a funny face at him. he giggles. TSERING looks at DESHAR. She pretends to be serious and so does PEMA.)*

TSERING: Yes. How can I help you?

RINPOCHE: Have her back. *(Pause.)* for a few days.

TSERING:

RINPOCHE:

TSERING: I did not send her.

RINPOCHE: She has broken the rules.

TSERING: Of?

RINPOCHE: Of the monastery. We have to set up a disciplinary... *(Pause.)*

RINPOCHE: We have an inspection.

TSERING: So?

RINPOCHE: We cannot have undisciplined nuns in the monastery.

TSERING: What did she do?

RINPOCHE: She was violent. *(Looks up at RINPOCHE.)* She hit a Chinese soldier and stole his uniform.

TSERING: You mean she was unruly. For a moment I thought she fought for something.

RINPOCHE: They will expel her and many others if we are seen as violent.

TSERING: Fighting for freedom is not violence. Misleading people is. If I was inspecting, I would have expelled a whole lot myself. *(Pause.)*

RINPOCHE: We need your help.

TSERING: Not my problem. *(Beat.)* Pema you continue *(PEMA and DESHAR keep making faces at each other and reacting to what the elders are talking about.)*

TSERING: Like I said. *(Loudly.)* PEMA.

PEMA: Teacher…yes teacher. I'm making corrections teacher.

TSERING *(Takes the paper.)* Here…what is this?

PEMA: It's the right word teacher. It isn't Mandarin,.

TSERING: Which is the verb and which is the object?

PEMA: Teacher… *(Looks at DESHAR.)*

TSERING: You girl…come here. Come and sit next to him *(DESHAR comes and sits next to PEMA.)*

TSERING: Help him.

DESHAR: This is the word and this is the object Pah-la. *(Pause.)*

TSERING: This is a grammar class. Not your family home.

DESHAR: I am sorry, Teacher Tsering.

TSERING: Why is this sentence incorrect? *(She looks at it again.)*

DESHAR:

TSERING: You can't *(Pause. Looks at RINPOCHE.)*

TSERING: Because Pema, in Tibetan languages verbs come after objects. And in Chinese usage it's the other way around. You get it?

PEMA: Yes, teacher Tsering.

TSERING: No...you don't. And neither do you *(At DESHAR.)* and nor will you. *(RINPOCHE.)*

Because deep deep inside all of you have become Chinese. Your mind is in Mandarin and you are just using Tibetan sounding words.

(To DESHAR.) You may leave.

RINPOCHE: They are children Tsering *(Pause.)*

TSERING: This one is mine and that girl, yours. Take her away.

RINPOCHE: I can't. Just for a week. Keep her here. *(Pause.)*

RINPOCHE: Her mind...it's not mature. We do not want her to do anything/

TSERING: Great education Rinpoche! Well done. *(Pause.)*

TSERING: Re-education is it? Is that what the Chinese are calling it?

RINPOCHE: Yes. They want to reduce the number of nuns in the monasteries.

TSERING: No. They want to save resources. That's what we are for them. Costs. *(Pause.)* and they are coming by the train isn't it. And look at the village, gearing up to celebrate the one day when the train will stop here. Idiots.

RINPOCHE: We do not have violence in our culture Tsering.

TSERING: Culture. *(Laughs.)* We were warriors Rinpoche. You are confused between culture and theology. These words

9

have meanings. They are not sounds you make every morning, while doing the Kora.

RINPOCHE: The monastery needs her to be out for a week. We have our hands full already.

TSERING: She left on her own. I have my hands full too. *(Pause.)*

RINPOCHE: She was meant for this path.

TSERING: Then let her be.

RINPOCHE: I don't want her to be expelled.

TSERING: You have destroyed her ability to judge right from wrong.

RINPOCHE: She ran away. From you. We found her.

TSERING: But you did not send her back home, did you? *(He looks at DESHAR.)*

RINPOCHE: It's for the village Tsering. It's a site of great learning. Do you deny that? *(Pause.)*

RINPOCHE: The village needs it *(Pause.)*

TSERING: If she makes one mistake, I will throw her out and leave her at your gates myself.

PEMA: *(Loudly.) SHE WILL STAY HERE (Looks down.)*

RINPOCHE: *(With folded hands.)* Thank you… Thank you Commander Tsering. *(Pause.)*

TSERING: You can sleep in the shed outside. No contact with the students.

DESHAR: Yes, teacher Tsering.

PEMA: I will bring her the food teacher.

TSERING: No you won't. I will. You won't meet her, see her or talk to her for this week... Is that clear? *(Pause.)* Is that clear?

DESHAR and PEMA: Yes teacher Tsering.

RINPOCHE: Thank you.

TSERING: I am not doing this for you. I am doing this for the village. *(Pause.)* I heard you have some prayer rituals to bless the train.

RINPOCHE: Yes. We have been asked.

TSERING: By?

RINPOCHE: The authorities.

TSERING: And what does his Holiness say about the Beijing Lhasa express.

RINPOCHE: He says it's just a vessel. It's not good or bad. It depends on how it's used and what it brings.

TSERING *(Laughs.)* A vessel! A vessel he says! A vessel that brings in the beast in its entirety is just a vessel! 'Just'. Unfortunately His Holiness only knows one meaning of the word Just. The one about fairness is lost on him.

RINPOCHE: He is the god of compassion.

TSERING: Yes. He is. But you see, my god of compassion has JUST escaped to India. I am stuck here. With all of you. *(Pause.)* Just stuck with all you train worshipping monks.

SCENE 3

Late Night. PEMA and DESHAR on a mountain. PEMA looking at the sky through a small telescope. There is some snow but it's not completely covered in snow.

PEMA: OOOOOO…where did you get it.

DESHAR: Tashi brought it.

PEMA: From?

DESHAR: Beijing.

PEMA: Nice. I want to be an astronaut when I grow up.
  (DESHAR laughs out aloud.)

PEMA: Look, that's an astronaut.

DESHAR *(Pretending to be serious.)* Where…where…is the astronaut?

PEMA: There…on that star. It's a new space ship.

DESHAR: What's a space ship?

PEMA: A space ship is the Yak on which astronauts go far.

DESHAR: How far?

PEMA: To another world. Look.

DESHAR: That's a Yak?

PEMA: No…that's a spaceship on the bright star. When I become a man, I will be the first Chinese on a star beyond that bright star.

DESHAR: Chinese?

PEMA: Tibetan. I mean Tibetan *(They hear the train. PEMA looks at the train in the distance through the telescope.)*

PEMA: Actually… I think, I will be an engine driver.

12

DESHAR: Oh… *(Laughs.)* Why?

PEMA: Look at the train *(DESHAR looks.)*

DESHAR: Beautiful. I have never seen it this closely. Is that a place to eat?

PEMA: Yes, it's called a Dining car.

DESHAR: How do you know?

PEMA: Dolma's father has been on it. He told me.

DESHAR: Wow it's nice.

PEMA: Show. *(Pause.)*

PEMA: I think I want to be a waiter. Look at his uniform.

DESHAR *(Playing him.)* Show me…have you seen the engine driver's uniform. Here.

PEMA: Yes…on second thoughts/

DESHAR: Yes, I think you will be a good engine driver.

PEMA: It's quite a fast train. I think I'll do a good job of it. How far is it?

DESHAR: Very far. It's a good telescope. There's a shepherd out at night.

PEMA: Where? *(Pause.)* Oh yes there.

DESHAR: I think his sheep are beautiful.

PEMA: Show me…yes he has so many.

DESHAR: They are climbing up quite quickly aren't they?

PEMA: Yes.

DESHAR: I think he is really brave, to go out at night.

PEMA: You think he is braver than the engine driver?

DESHAR: nd the waiter, and the astronaut.

PEMA: Actually…I think/

DESHAR: You are already a shepherd Pema *(Laughs.)*

PEMA *(Smiles.)* Yes.

DESHAR: So what do you want to be when you grow up?

PEMA: I want to be this.

DESHAR: No improvement.

PEMA: No. Why can't I be this? I like this.

DESHAR: That's because you haven't seen the world outside.

PEMA: I just did. I saw it, and I think I am fine.

DESHAR: You don't want to move ahead?

PEMA: I am ahead.

DESHAR: If the Buddha thought like this, he would never have become the Buddha.

PEMA: The Buddha did not have a telescope. *(They laugh.)*

DESHAR: What if they don't let you be who you are Pema.

PEMA: Who?

DESHAR: The Chinese.

PEMA: Will they not let you be a nun?

DESHAR: They want all of us to be like them. *(The train passes by with a loud sound. They look at it.)*

PEMA: It's beautiful.

DESHAR: And yet.

PEMA: And yet, I want to be a shepherd and you want to be a nun. *(Laughs.)*

DESHAR: Dorjee is a nun. I am an imposter.

PEMA: What's an imposter?

DESHAR: Someone who pretends to be someone else.

PEMA: Then what are you really?

DESHAR: I don't know.

PEMA: Look...look through this. *(DESHAR looks all around.)*

PEMA: What do you want to be?

DESHAR: I don't want to be an imposter.

PEMA: Yes, but what do you like? What do you want to be?

DESHAR: I want to be...a star. That star.

PEMA: How is that possible.

DESHAR: I don't know. I really don't know what I want to be.

PEMA: Did the Buddha become a star?

DESHAR: He became everything and nothing, at once.
(Pause.)

PEMA: I want to be a shepherd. It's better. *(DESHAR laughs.)*

(Suddenly she stops laughing. TSERING appears.)

(Silence.)

TSERING: Pema. Come here *(PEMA goes running to TSERING and stands next to him apologetically. TSERING slaps him hard. He falls.)*

DESHAR: I am sorry...I am really/

15

TSERING: Did I grant you permission to take him?

DESHAR: No...no...I am really sorry/

TSERING: Did I ask you to leave the house and join a nunnery? *(Silence.)*

TSERING: You go when you want, you come back when you want, you do whatever you feel like and I am the poor father am I?

DESHAR: Pahla, I am sorry, I /

TSERING: I fought for this country Deshar. And His Holiness called my movement off by turning non violent one day. And the whole world just forgot about us. I brought you up, by myself with everything I could and you just left.

DESHAR: You killed Amahla. *(Pause.)*

TSERING: What?

DESHAR: You killed her.

TSERING: No Deshar, I gave her dignity. She was going to leave me, and go away to meet his holiness with my baby in her arms, across these mountains. She was fleeing her home to seek the blessings of a man who called off our only chance of independence.

DESHAR: So you killed her.

TSERING:

DESHAR: You shot her.

TSERING: I shot her? Who said I shot her?

DESHAR: The villagers. Everyone knows.

TSERING: She was brought back, raped and dying in an army truck. You were lying on the floor of the truck.

DESHAR: And then you shot her.

TSERING: They said I could only save one of you Deshar. Your mother asked me to shoot her *(Pause.)*

TSERING: WE…we, your mother and I saved you Deshar. *(Pause.)*

DESHAR: That's not what everyone says Pahla. That is not what people believe.

TSERING: I don't lie Deshar. There is no one more Buddhist than me in the world.

DESHAR: But people/

TSERING: People believe his holiness wants independence Deshar, when he himself has announced that he does not… People believe, what they want to believe.

DESHAR: You should have saved her. I was an infant. *(Silence.)*

TSERING: You know what the real problem with Tibet is Deshar? *(Pause.)* Its not the Chinese.

It's our children. They grow up to be delusional.

DESHAR:

TSERING: Spare this boy. Go back to the nunnery.

DESHAR:

DESHAR: You…you are a cynical, old, angry man Pah-la! You will make him like yourself.

TSERING: Come Pema…we do not need to stand here and listen to this. *(He begins to walk away.)*

DESHAR: You killed her Pah-la… You killed her… *(DESHAR breaks down.)* Everyone knows you killed her Pah-la. *(She falls down and starts crying.)*

(Pause.)

TSERING *(Goes back to her.)* You will never ever call me that. Is that clear? Your mother died. I am sorry. But she was born in Tibet. And in Tibet, your mother's death, your father's anger are not the only things hindering your salvation. *(Silence.)*

DESHAR:

TSERING: And you will never ever come close to this boy. *(Silence.)*

TSERING: You don't know what you want to be isn't it? Isnt that what she said?

PEMA:

TSERING: What?

PEMA: Yes…yes Teacher Tsering.

TSERING: Go back. Get re-educated. Get humiliated by the Chinese soldiers and keep hoping that His Holiness will reappear one day and make everything alright. This delusion is what you ran away for, isn't it?.

DESHAR: I ran away from you. You killed my mother. *(Pause.)*

TSERING: If you don't know who you are, living in Tibet, you will never know who you are Deshar. Its much easier to be a Buddha than to be an ordinary Tibetan in this world. *(He takes PEMA and walks off.)*

SCENE 4

RINPOCHE and the Nuns of the monastery, alternately light and blow out butter lamps. They chant as they engage in this ritual. A brilliant light on stage, with the glow of 100 butter lamps, and at any point of time most lamps are lit while no lamp is lit long enough. The continuous play of the temporality of fire and life is played through this ritual.

Sound of the train. As the train arrives closer, the nuns and RINPOCHE turn to look at the train. As the train arrives at a high speed, the lamps go off. Darkness.

SCENE 5

A giant Buddha statue.

The prayer room and main class room in the Nunnery.

One chair which CONSTABLE GAPHEL has placed. DENG is looking at the statue. Next to it are Buddhist scriptures and also materials for prayers.

RINPOCHE is looking at DENG.

There is a flip board next to the chair.

DENG: How much does it cost us Rinpoche?

RINPOCHE: Sorry?

DENG: How much is this Buddha statue for? What is the damage to the common tax payer, such as myself?

RINPOCHE: 1400 years, commander Deng. The tax payers of this country have got a really good bargain.

DENG *(Smiles.)* No one. Absolutely no one can defeat Buddhist monks at rhetoric.

RINPOCHE: Blessings of the Buddha.

DENG: I love your sense of humour.

RINPOCHE: One wants to smile. The Buddha laughed a lot.

DENG: The Buddha. THE BUDDHA…must have been a great fundraiser.

RINPOCHE: On the contrary it was a cultural revolution.

DENG: *(RINPOCHE smiles.)*

DENG: How is it that the Cultural revolution spared these relics? Chairman Mao must have really liked them. *(Pause.)*

RINPOCHE: Would you like some tea?

DENG: Is that your trunk?

RINPOCHE: Yes.

DENG: What is in it?

RINPOCHE: You may take a look.

DENG: Nothing personal I hope. *(As DENG walks to the trunk to examine it.)*

RINPOCHE: Personal? No…nothing outside the person. *(DENG opens it. Its empty. DENG shows it to him. RINPOCHE smiles.)*

DENG: Where are the contents of this?

RINPOCHE: It's an empty box.

DENG: Where is the stuff that was in it?

RINPOCHE: Gave it away.

DENG: When?

RINPOCHE: Over this lifetime.

DENG: We'll know. Gaphel, please look. *(RINPOCHE smiles at GAPHEL. GAPHEL bows.)*

DENG: We have Tibetans working for the motherland.

RINPOCHE: Surely. Gaphel-la, *(To the CONSTABLE.)* just put back everything in its place please. Especially the scriptures.

(TO DENG.) WE ARE SHORT OF PEOPLE AS YOU KNOW.

DENG: I think that you are far too many to be honest.

These scriptures. How old are they?

RINPOCHE: Thousands of years.

DENG: New books?

RINPOCHE: Several.

DENG: Who writes them?

RINPOCHE: Scholars. Monks and Nuns.

DENG: What are they about?

RINPOCHE: The mind.

DENG: The Mind?

RINPOCHE: Yes, all of Buddhism is only about one thing. The mind.

DENG: And?

RINPOCHE: And?

DENG: Separatism? False history?

RINPOCHE: I'm afraid not. We are yet to find our political teeth.

DENG *(To CONSTABLE.)* Nothing?

CONSTABLE: Nothing commander.

DENG: Why did you give everything away?

RINPOCHE: I gained a little, very little knowledge. It left no place for things.

DENG: So what are the pillars of your education?

RINPOCHE: The 'what' of our education?

DENG: Pillars…foundation, principles? What do you teach… about the mind?

RINPOCHE: Pillar *(Pause.)* To see the world for what it is.

DENG: And which is?

RINPOCHE: It's in our mind. Isn't it?

DENG:

RINPOCHE: It is. In our mind.

DENG: This chair. It's here.

RINPOCHE: Yes, in a way.

DENG: In what way.

RINPOCHE: In the way, that I first have to perceive of myself in my mind and then perceive of this chair through my sense of 'I'. That if 'I am here' then there is a chair. Surely.

DENG: If you are here then it is here. But it costs money. It costs tax payers money to get this chair here. Or is the money too in our mind?

RINPOCHE: In a way, it is actually.

DENG: So while shepherd and nomads in your village starve to send the monastery food and blankets, you question

22

whether the things they are giving you are really here or not? This is your education?

RINPOCHE:

DENG: This Buddha statue, it costs a few thousand Yuans. These robes they cost us money. This monastery is not running on your mind, it's working on labour and money.

RINPOCHE: That is true as well. Just like the police force is.

DENG: Oh…the Police force. The Police force protects. What does the monastery protect?

RINPOCHE: What does the police force protect?

DENG: People. Common people.

RINPOCHE: From?

DENG: Other people.

RINPOCHE: Why?

DENG: Why?.

RINPOCHE: So what does it protect exactly, in people?

DENG: Their life.

RINPOCHE: Which is?

DENG: Their happiness, their well being, their way of life.

RINPOCHE: I am really glad Commander Deng. It seems like you and I have the same job. *(Pause.)*

DENG: Your people need re-education.

RINPOCHE: I see.

DENG: Your knowledge is of no use to the common man. People cannot be starving while hundreds of monks and nuns, sit in monasteries and debate whether they are really here or not.

RINPOCHE: Do you realize Commander Deng, that people have never starved in Tibet. They have however in mainland China. *(Pause.)*

DENG: I am not here to play word games with you.

RINPOCHE: I was merely clarifying.

DENG: We do not discuss economics with Monks!

RINPOCHE: Why?

DENG: Because you consume material and look down upon the material condition.

RINPOCHE: We do not look down upon any condition. On the contrary, the Buddha pushed for land reforms.

DENG: I am a soldier, not a monk. I don't wake up every morning and debate.

RINPOCHE: Hmm…and we are not even wondering who really needs the re-education *(Pause.)*

DENG: Constable *(CONSTABLE GAPHEL turns the flip chart.)*

DENG: So, these are our five major pillars of re-education. The education of those who were denied it when they were young. Read.

(GAPHEL looks uncertain. GAPHEL folds his hands and takes permission from RINPOCHE.)

GAPHEL: *(Reads tentatively.)* One. Opposition to Separatism.

Two. Unity of Tibet and China.

Three. Recognition of the Chinese Government appointed/

(DENG places his hand on GAPHEL's shoulder on noticing his discomfort.)

Three. Recognition of the Chinese Government appointed Panchen Lama as the true Panchen Lama.

Four. Agreement that the Dalai Lama is a political terrorist dressed up in the garb of a religious man and that he is destroying the unity of the Motherland.

Five. To agree that Tibet was never and shall never be a separate country and it is in fact an integral part of our beloved motherland.

RINPOCHE: Excellent.

DENG: Do you agree?

RINPOCHE: With?

DENG: The five pillars *(RINPOCHE goes closer to the flip chart.)*

RINPOCHE: Too many nouns unfortunately. My entire training is in verbs. *(Pause.)*

DENG: You need to include these pillars in your morning assembly. Every day.

RINPOCHE: The nunnery will not do any such thing.

DENG: Then you will have no nuns to teach.

RINPOCHE: This is a school of philosophy commander Deng, not a shop in downtown Beijing. There is going to be no bargain.

DENG: Well, in that case your students will need to put up with some harsh re-education.

RINPOCHE: May the Buddha make us see each other's views.

DENG: May the Buddha stop breeding separatists.

25

RINPOCHE: There are no separatists here *(Pause.)*

(DENG, signaLING to CONSTABLE to go out and bring someone.)

(Tense silence between RINPOCHE and DENG. DESHAR is brought in. She stands in a corner and bows to RINPOCHE. She is angry.)

DENG: I suppose we know, who this girl is. *(Silence. GAPHEL hands him a file.)*

DENG: Deshar Tsering. Daughter of Ngabo Tsering. Commander, Chushi Gangdruk. Trained in Colorado by CIA. *(Pause.)* No separatists?

RINPOCHE:

DESHAR: I am sorry Rinpoche. I was home but/

DENG: Constable Gaphel. Do we have any other information about her father?

GAPHEL: No…no commander.

DESHAR: He has nothing to do with me. I am not his daughter.

RINPOCHE: Deshar! *(DESHAR looks down. Sobs.)*

RINPOCHE: You can go to your room.

DESHAR: I am sorry. I am sorry Rinpoche.

RINPOCHE: You may go. We can speak /

DENG: I don't think you should actually. *(Silence.)*

DENG: Perhaps you can help us understand if we need reeducation or not?

RINPOCHE: She is a young nun. Her education is not complete. Let her go.

DENG: I thought she is one of your best. *(Looking at the file.)*

RINPOCHE: Yes.

DENG: if she answers our questions satisfactorily, we will let everyone stay here and there will be no re-education. *(Pause.)* Alright?

RINPOCHE: Deshar, you may/

DENG: You may not Deshar, if you want to give a chance to your sisters to stay.

DESHAR *(Looks up at him sternly.)* Ask.

DENG: The Buddha meets a blacksmith. The Blacksmith works eighteen hours a day to make a living. The Buddha asks for his tools in return for salvation. What should the blacksmith do?

RINPOCHE: Go Deshar

(DESHAR begins to go away.)

DENG: Are these your best students? Really?

RINPOCHE: She does not know the answer to…

DENG: Then how do we justify the support Rinpoche, when your best cannot answer /

DESHAR: The Blacksmith should not have to work 18 hours a day to make a living. If despite knowing this, the Buddha asks for his tools, the Blacksmith should break every bone in the Buddha's body. *(Pause.)*

RINPOCHE: Go Deshar.

DENG: The Blacksmith had two children, out of whom one died due to an illness that could not be treated. There is one building in the village which is the monastery of the Buddha. The Blacksmith goes to the Buddha and pleads for a hospital while his second child is unwell.

27

The Buddha insists on the importance of Salvation and wants to keep the monastery. The blacksmith gathers other people in the village to plead but the Buddha still does not hear them. He keeps insisting on the monastery and makes the case for Salvation, what should the blacksmith do.

DESHAR: The Blacksmith should start a revolution. Overthrow the Buddha and take over the monastery.

DENG: *(Looks at RINPOCHE.)* Well… *(Looks at DESHAR.)*

DENG: Good. I must meet your father before I leave.

DESHAR: One day, a man steals the blacksmiths clothes. He wears them and roams around the neighbouring towns and villages, claiming to be a blacksmith by the day but by the night destroying every house that gave him shelter. Soon he claims that every house is his and that all of them are one without any difference whatsoever as long as the similarity is in their allegiance to this blacksmith who actually is not a Blacksmith at all in the first place.

One day the imposter enters the original Blacksmith's house, tries to throw him and his family out, breaks the altar of their god. The original Blacksmith and his family are asked to now prove to the imposter that they are loyal imposters and the imposter is the original Blacksmith.

The original Blacksmith and his family still have their tools in their hands and are mighty good at using them.

What should the Blacksmith do? *(Pause.)*

RINPOCHE: Deshar go in. Now! *(DENG comes close to her.)*

DENG: Do I sense a streak of violence? Did you get it from your father or is it part of monastic education nowadays?

DESHAR *(Makes a fist holding herself back.)* What should the blacksmith do? *(Pause.)*

DENG *(To DESHAR.)* Re-education starts tomorrow. For everyone. *(Pause.)*

Rinpoche: There is a contradiction in your education.

DENG: Which is?

RINPOCHE: You are protecting people from yourselves.

DENG: There is one in your education as well Rinpoche.

RINPOCHE:

DENG: You are not sure whether you are here or not, but you are absolutely sure that Tibet is yours.

RINPOCHE:

DENG *(Loudly.)* Re-education starts tomorrow at 4 am constable. Let us show the master and his nuns, who is here and who exists only in their minds.

SCENE 6

Montage of the next three days and nights.

The same room as Scene 5.

The Buddha statue is present. In front of it many more chairs as the nuns are being brought in, told to write, learn, repeat. They are made to read newspapers and mark lines. They are asked to stand up and sing the National Anthem.

They get exhausted but are being brought in over and over again.

29

SCENE 7

Same room. Three nights later. Nuns are sitting exhausted, in a corner. RINPOCHE is on the floor lying in front of the Buddha statue with his eyes shut. There are newspapers strewn around. DENG is walking, picking up newspaper after newspaper and looking at them.

He looks at RINPOCHE.

DENG: There isn't one who has marked anything in green. Not one. *(Looks around.)*

For three days and three nights we are here. In other nunneries, we have done this in two days and moved on. You have to mark everything you believe in green and what you believe has to be for the good of the motherland. What is the problem? What are the nuns in this nunnery finding so hard to believe?

DESHAR: The newspapers are yours. They are lying.

DENG: And you? Do you not understand that all your sisters here will be expelled if the re-education is unsuccessful?.

DESHAR: If it is successful, there won't be any need to expel us. Feed him.

RINPOCHE: I am fine.

DENG: You, you have taught them to disbelieve. In Sera, Drepung, Ganden Monasteries we have had many who we have been able to save. But here, your influence is complete. Total!.

RINPOCHE: I don't know how you forced the other monks and nuns. When I see this nunnery and its quest for truth, it makes me proud. *(Pause.)*

DENG: Dorjee. *(DORJEE stands up in panic.)*

DENG: Please bring it. *(DORJEE remains standing.)*

DENG: Where is it? *(Loudly.)*

(DORJEE pulls out a folded photograph.)

DENG: Can you please let your sisters and your master know what it is. Now.

DORJEE *(Tentatively.)* It's a photo.

DENG: Of? *(DORJEE remains quiet.)*

(DENG looks at her.)

DORJEE: His Holiness the Dalai Lama *(CONSTABLE GAPHEL immediately bows. DENG looks at him. He stands up.)*

DENG: And it was found in? *(DORJEE remains quite.)*

RINPOCHE: I gave it to her. When her brother died. For solace.

DENG: Do we not know in this country, it's illegal? *(Pause.)*

DENG: Nun Dorjee, you have your licence. You may leave this nunnery and be a nun elsewhere *(DORJEE starts to cry.)*

DENG: You may leave. There is a train tonight. Take it and leave this place. This nunnery is shut.

DORJEE: I need the money. I need the money Rinpoche, I'll starve otherwise *(DORJEE cries holding RINPOCHE.)*

RINPOCHE: I understand. *(Takes the picture.)* Keep this face in your mind. Go…go my dear.

DORJEE: But where will I go Rinpoche.

RINPOCHE: Take that train. It's a vessel, like His Holiness said. It won't make you less Tibetan or less Buddhist. Take it and go somewhere far. Search for the Buddha in you. *(Smiles.)*

(Looks at DENG.)

31

RINPOCHE: So is our nunnery going to be closed?

DENG: Since this is your education *(Looking at the newspapers.)* I am afraid yes. We will break it and build a hospital.

RINPOCHE: May the Buddha bless you for building a hospital *(Silence.)*

RINPOCHE: It has already been /

DENG: The demolition on the east side, should begin any moment.

RINPOCHE: I thought, you were bringing in equipment to build a road.

DENG: To the hospital. *(RINPOCHE turns towards the nuns.)*

RINPOCHE: My dear sisters in the path of the Buddha. There is no licence that anyone can give from you, for your journey on the path of salvation. You may not be allowed in a nunnery again but the Buddha is within us. It is to be awakened. Leave.

DENG: Everyone in a straight line. Leave the building.

(RINPOCHE goes and sits next to the Buddha statue.)

DENG: Everyone in a straight line. Leave the building.

GAPHEL *(Goes to RINPOCHE.)* Rinpoche, master, please…

RINPOCHE: Everyone in a straight line. Leave the building.

DENG: Leave. *(RINPOCHE turns to face him.)*

RINPOCHE: I will go with him. Let the machines arrive. *(Silence.)*

GAPHEL: Master…please.

DENG: Leave. *(RINPOCHE holds the Buddha's feet tightly and sits.)*

(Starts chanting "Om mani padme hum".)

(Gradually the nuns all come close to RINPOCHE, chanting "Om mani padme hum".)

(DENG looks at them. He tries to drag RINPOCHE gradually to safety.)

GAPHEL: Commander...I'll ask him commander...Rinpoche, master, this is good for everyone, please, please.

(All the nuns chant louder. DESHAR's eyes are open. Others have shut their eyes and are chanting. RINPOCHE chants with his eyes shut and hands folded as DENG tries to drag him out with the CONSTABLE joining in trying to do it respectfully.)

(DESHAR aggressively goes to DENG. Holds his collar and stands. He stands fixed, stoic.)

RINPOCHE *(Loudly.)* DESHAR!! *(Everyone goes quiet.)*

(RINPOCHE comes in between and stops her.)

You cannot...cannot hate him Deshar. You cannot be a learned Buddhist scholar, and hate this man who is being cruel to you right now. He is a Buddha too *(Pause. RINPOCHE goes to DENG, to help him get up.)*

We can lose this nunnery, we can lose our land, our language but Deshar...we are this... *(Pointing at the Buddha.)* This is our path.

If we become violent, we lose everything.

My child you cannot, cannot hate.

(DESHAR falls down crying.)

RINPOCHE: Leave, everyone. Leave. I am too old to now go out into the world. Let me go with my Buddha. Please leave *(GAPHEL is on the floor. RINPOCHE goes close to him.)*

33

RINPOCHE: I am at peace. Please leave. *(GAPHEL sits with folded hands.)*

May I teach my last lesson? *(DENG walks away.)*

(Looks at his students, hands folded.) The Sermon of fire. Everything Burns. Everything always burns, and the world is never the same. We never see the same mountain twice, or the same forest, for in our minds we are burning.

Have patience, let the fire of knowledge burn and the fire of hatred douse itself. Understand that everything changes and this too shall pass. Don't hate. Don't hate. I complete my teachings now. I hope what you are about to see, does not make you hate this man and rather you can be compassionate towards his suffering that has led him here.

May the Buddha be with you.

(RINPOCHE goes and sits at the feet of the Buddha. CONSTABLE GAPHEL goes closer. He is unable to touch him. The nuns walk away with hands folded. DESHAR remains close to RINPOCHE.)

SCENE 8

A month later. Snow all around. DESHAR is standing with a can of petrol. Some wood to light a fire. She standing resolute looking out. She is looking far. PEMA enters from behind and looks at her. He pulls out his telescope. Looks far.

PEMA: That is...it.

DESHAR: *(Startled.)*

PEMA: The last of the debris.

(DESHAR snatches the telescope and is about to look. Stops. Gives it back.)

DESHAR: They broke everything?.

34

PEMA: Yes. *(Pause.)*

PEMA *(Looks at the sky.)* It took a month. Was a big nunnery. *(Pause.)*

DESHAR: What are you doing here? At this time of the night? Go home.

PEMA: I come here everyday. To wave at the train. Sometimes they wave back *(They smile at each other.)*

DESHAR: Go Pema. It's late.

PEMA: I'll go once the train passes. Where have you been?

DESHAR: Outside the nunnery.

PEMA: The whole month?

(DESHAR nods.)

PEMA: I looked for you. They didn't let me close to the site.

DESHAR: I know.

(Pause.)

DESHAR: Pah-la?

PEMA: He has not stepped out since they started the demolition of the monastery.

DESHAR: I thought he hated it.

PEMA: Everyday he did the Kora. He has a picture of his holiness hidden in the rice box.

DESHAR:

PEMA: Do you hate something sister? *(Long pause.)*

DESHAR: You?

PEMA: Grammar. *(They laugh.)*

DESHAR: What do you hate about grammar Pema.

PEMA: It's a lot of work and I don't understand it. *(Pause.)* I think we hate that which we do not understand.

DESHAR: *(Looking up at him surprised.)* Pema, you're a scholar. *(Laughs.)*

PEMA: I told teacher Tsering the same thing in class the other day.

DESHAR: You did?

PEMA: He gave me sweets. The next day. But I knew he gave it to me for saying this, about hate.

DESHAR: How?

PEMA: How what?

DESHAR: How do you know, he gave you the sweets for something you said the previous day?

PEMA: I understand things immediately. He takes a day. *(DESHAR laughs.)*

What is this? *(Pointing at the petrol.)*

DESHAR: We need wood. Go, get some

PEMA: I can't get wood. I have to see the train and go home.

DESHAR: You go home then.

PEMA: But I want to see the train.

DESHAR: Don't tonight. *(Pause.)* Pah-la will be worried for you.

PEMA: He is teaching. He thinks I am in the barn.

DESHAR: You have to stop lying Pema.

PEMA: I didn't hurt anyone.

DESHAR: You lied.

PEMA: One day a monk was roving in the forest, and a deer ran past him. Soon after a hunter who was chasing the deer, stopped next to him and asked about the deer. Is there truth in telling where the deer is, or is there truth in saving a life?.

DESHAR: *(Laughs.)* Truth is to tell where the deer is but yes morally the monk might as well lie.

PEMA: Well, how can the monk tell where the deer is sister? By the time he says it, the deer would have moved. No one knows where someone else is exactly. There is no truth that the monk can say. *(Pause.)*

DESHAR *(In awe of him.)* What are you learning Pema!

PEMA: Tibetan. *(He looks through his telescope.)* It'll be here soon *(Smiles.)*

DESHAR: How far is it? *(She gets up.)*

PEMA: Other side of two mountains.

 (Pause.)

DESHAR: Let's have a race?

PEMA: Ok? *(Pause.)* Where are we racing to? *(Small pause.)*

DESHAR: To the top of that hill.

PEMA: But we'll miss the train.

DESHAR: First horn we start running, by the fifth horn we need to get there. Whoever gets there first, gets to go to the mastiff show in Kham.

PEMA: The Big Mastiff show?

DESHAR: Yes, the big one.

PEMA: But I want to see the train.

DESHAR: Or the big mastiff show?

PEMA: Ok I'll see the train tomorrow.

DESHAR: Good decision.

PEMA: The first horn will be, when it's one mountain bend away. *(He looks.)*

DESHAR: Great.

PEMA: Don't be angry if you lose.

DESHAR: I won't be, but you have to cross the top of the hill by five horns. Only then.

PEMA: Yes.

DESHAR: And don't turn back.

PEMA: Yes. Will you be angry if I turn back.

DESHAR: NO!

PEMA: Good to ask both of you. *(Laughs.)*

DESHAR: I am not like him.

PEMA *(Laughs loudly.)* You are the same person sister! His grammar is better. *(Pause.)* Ok here it is.

Deshar: How far?

PEMA: One more bend.

DESHAR: Pema...what is anger?.

PEMA: I am going to win this race.

DESHAR: Do you know?

PEMA: Anger is to forget that, you, me, the mountain, the train and the fire that we would have lit if he had wood, are all one. Anger is the illusion of separation. *(He laughs.)*

DESHAR: What? *(First horn.)*

(PEMA makes a face and runs.)

DESHAR: What did you say? *(PEMA has started running.)*

DESHAR: Tell Pah-la, I love him *(Second horn. PEMA turns.)*

DESHAR: Don't look back *(PEMA runs. Third horn. DESHAR pours petrol on herself. Begins to chant. Fourth horn she lights herself. Fifth horn, she walks on the track. The chant fills the space. She lights herself. The train blows its horn incessantly. DESHAR burns.)*

INTERVAL.

ACT 2

SCENE 1

A week later from end of Act 1… Inspector DENG walks, in to his house in Lhasa. There is smoke outside seen through the window. JIA is sitting on the bed. There is a television. A large picture of Mao Tse Tung and a small one of their daughter Liu. She is about to head out the moment she sees him. He stops her.

JIA: Move…

DENG: No… no…Jia/ *(JIA tries to push him and move, he holds her back and pushes her forcefully, so that she falls on the bed.)*

DENG: Jia! *(Silence.)*

JIA: Where is she?

DENG: Ok…I am sorry? I am trying. The entire police force is/ *(Pause.)*

JIA: let me go.

DENG: You cannot go out, in the middle of this /

JIA: Ask your guards to let me go Deng.

DENG: They'll burn you alive.

JIA *(Loudly.)* WHERE IS SHE DENG? WHERE IS OUR DAUGHTER LIU? *(Silence.)*

DENG *(Sits down.)* I am trying to find her.

JIA: You have not stepped out of the prison in 3 days Deng.

DENG: We got the nun.

JIA: She's alive?

DENG: Yes. She was found, burnt badly, by the authorities in Kham.

JIA: You found her. You can't find your daughter.

DENG: She started the riots.

JIA: She burnt herself. They are burning others.

DENG: These Tibetans are savages.

JIA: Our daughter is missing.

DENG: I sent a search party.

JIA: Where?

DENG: To the school.

JIA: And?

DENG: They couldn't get there.

JIA: Why?

DENG: I had to change their order. There was rioting around the Potala Palace.

JIA: So you changed the orders of those who were going to look for your daughter?

DENG: I had orders.

JIA: From?

DENG: Beijing.

JIA: Who in Beijing?

DENG: From Beijing. From Beijing!

JIA: There is no person is there? You take your orders from a city. *(Pause.)*

DENG: Have you heard from anyone else?

JIA: Who?

DENG: Any of the other parents?

JIA: Her school bus didn't come back.

DENG: She'll be alright. I know. *(JIA gets up, pulls DENG to the window.)*

JIA: What's that soot in the air Inspector Deng? It's coming from the Chinese quarters.

DENG: Liu…my daughter…my daughter is /

JIA: Missing. And you have locked me in this house with these two guards at the door.

DENG: It is for your protection.

JIA: Well, thank you very much. Now ask them to move. I have a daughter to look for. *(DENG's phone rings.)*

JIA: Don't pick up.

DENG:

JIA: Don't *(DENG takes the call.)*

DENG: Yes comrade. I am here. *(Pause.)* Yes comrade. Is she? Yes I am coming. We will find out. It wasn't me, no comrade. I tried to contain it but …yes…yes.

(JIA begins to move out. DENG keeps blocking her path.)

Yes…comrade…I am coming. I'll have the confession. Any day now.
My daughter…she is…No…no comrade, I am coming… yes…for the motherland/

(JIA takes his phone throws it on the ground and smashes it.)

(Silence.)

JIA:

DENG: I'll look for her Jia. The entire police force, with all its /

JIA: You...you inspector Deng, pushed someone's daughter to burn herself. This is your price. And as always, I have to pay for it as well. *(JIA lights a cigarette. She coughs.)*

DENG: I don't think you should be smoking in this /

JIA: I'll burn the house down.

DENG: Jia.

JIA: One by one... everything.

DENG: I know she is ok. *(He is almost in tears.)*

JIA: Bullshit. *(DENG's other phone rings.)*

DENG: Comrade...yes... I got it. I'll be there comrade. *(He begins to leave.)*

JIA: You're playing that game again.

DENG: What game?

JIA: Comrade fuck me... fuck me comrade. *(DENG walks up to her and holds her tightly.)*

DENG: The party is going to take action against me Jia, if she does not confess.

JIA: Who?

DENG: The nun.

JIA: To what?

DENG: To doing it on the orders of the Dalai Lama.

43

JIA: Your daughter is missing, and you are beating up a half
burnt nun to get a confession for your party?

DENG: I don't hit women. *(JIA claps and is ready to leave with
her purse.)*

DENG: No no no...Jia...please.

JIA: you wont be able to find my daughter Deng. You are not
a person. You are a system. Systems don't have children.

DENG: I need to get my name cleared. Else we are all
finished. I'm doing it for the family.

JIA: Asshole.

DENG: Come with me. I'll take you somewhere safe and I'll
find her.

JIA: And so will I. *(Pause.)*

DENG: You'll die in a day.

JIA: You're dead already. *(JIA takes out her lipstick. puts it on
Mao Tse Tung's photo.)*

JIA: It's red.

DENG: I love you. don't do this.

JIA: Marxists should not get married. Should not have
children. You should sleep with each other.

DENG: Jia please! *(JIA takes her daughter's picture out of the
frame.)*

JIA: I am going to look for her. Myself. You can keep looking
for him.

DENG: I don't have time for this. *(Pause.)* Listen... let's try to
find her together.

JIA: If I don't find her. I will come back and burn this house before I get back to Beijing.

DENG: We decided together to come here.

JIA: No. you did.

DENG: That's a lie.

JIA: The whole thing is a lie. *(Pause.)*

(JIA takes out a knife from her purse.)

JIA: Ask your guards to move Deng. Else I'll slit my throat at the door. I promise you. *(She begins to walk out.)*

DENG: Jia...where are you going!! Where do you think you are just walking out into... do you know what's going on in the city...The Tibetans are killing Hans everywhere. Jia... !

JIA: I thought you were a good father Deng. But really... if you can burn someone else's daughter, what can one expect of you.

DENG: I didn't burn her. I wasn't even there. It's been a month.

JIA: You want to know, why she did it?

DENG:

JIA: Thank your stars she is a Buddhist nun. If your soldiers had demolished my home, I would have come to Lhasa, the very next day and...burnt you.

(Pause.) You want me to go or die at the door?

DENG: Please...please Jia. *(JIA places the knife on her throat. Begins to make a cut.)*

(DENG rushes and stops her. Throws the knife.)

45

DENG: Go. *(Pause.)* I can't force you to do anything.

JIA: Why?

DENG: Because... I love you.

JIA: No... because you are a soft communist. A revolutionary with a greeting card for a heart. First you are stern and then you repent it. You lead other people's children to death and then don't have to courage to find your own.

There's no place in this world for you Deng.

(The television suddenly starts playing some loud happy adverts. JIA looks at it. Looks at DENG. She picks up the television and drops it. It breaks.)

JIA: This is telling you nothing comrade.Go to the prison and watch life pass by. Tell that girl, she has changed Tibet forever. It doesn't take long for people to get to others, when they begin to burn themselves.

DENG: I will find Liu. Jia I will.

JIA: No Deng. You will get obsessed with getting a confession. Day and night. That's what you will do.

DENG: We are not looking for a confession Jia. We are looking for the truth!

JIA: It already sounds false when you say it in your party voice.

DENG: I...I am looking for the truth.

JIA: I am looking for my daughter Inspector Deng. There is only one of that. *(Pause.)*

DENG: If you find her, will you let me know.

JIA: No.

DENG:

JIA: If I don't, I will. Every night, in your worst nightmare.
(JIA walks out. DENG keeps sitting on the bed.)

SCENE 2

(Lhasa Central Prison. Late night. LING 30, is with DESHAR and
DENG. Polygraph room. DESHAR is in an interrogation chair. There
are two more chairs kept away from the interrogation chair. DESHAR
is plugged in to three monitors. One checks the dilation of her eyes.
Another her blood pressure. The third her sweat levels. There is a big
speaker and a light that goes green for truth, red for lies as the machine
changes measure.)

DENG: You received orders from his office in India?.

DESHAR:

DENG: Does she know?.

LING: Yes.

DENG: Why isn't she speaking?

LING (To DESHAR.) The Polygraph is on. Beep for lies, No
beep for truth.

DENG: Silence is registered as a lie. Manually. (DESHAR looks
at DENG.)

DENG: We want the truth. The truth.

DESHAR:

DENG: Was it a telegram or a phone call?.

DESHAR:

DENG: Are you writing?

LING: Yes sir.

47

DENG: Water. *(LING makes her drink water forcibly.)*

DENG: Who was it? Who asked you to?.

DESHAR:

DENG: Sing.

DESHAR: *(Feebly chants om mani padme hum.)*

DENG: An unconscious man was stabbed and set on fire
    by Tibetans, on the street next to the Potala Palace this
    morning.

DESHAR: *(Continues to chant. The monitors keep showing changes
    in her levels but there are no beeps.)*

DENG: A mob of Tibetan children burnt down an old
    woman's Tailoring shop with her locked inside it. This
    much fire. This is what you've done.

DESHAR: *(Shuts her eyes tightly and chants.)*

DENG: Sing with me. *(DENG sings 'for the motherland.)*

    (LING joins in.)

DENG: What is the problem in singing? Sing! *(DESHAR looks
    at him.)*

DENG: Sing or I'll wake everyone up and make them sing
    standing in the cold outside. *(DESHAR feebly sings.)*

DENG: Louder. *(DESHAR tries to sing louder.)*

DENG: Spit. *(DESHAR spits on her robe.)*

DENG: Clean. *(DESHAR cleans it with the cloth in her hand. She
    looks exhausted.)*

DENG: Who sent you orders to burn yourself?

DESHAR:

DENG: What about the Muslims? The Hui? Why are Tibetans attacking them? Did the Dalai Lama send orders to kill Muslims as well?

DESHAR (Chants.)

DENG: Who are you praying to? *(DESHAR keeps chanting.)*

DENG: Spit.

DESHAR: No one. *(The polygraph registers an answer with a green light. Does not beep.)*

DENG: Sing.

DESHAR: No one. *(The polygraph registers an answer with a green light. Does not beep.)*

DENG: What no one? *(DESHAR looks at him... silence.)*

DENG: Water *(LING throws water on her face, makes her drink water forcibly.)*

DENG: You received a call from the hotline in the Kirti Monastery. There are reports.

DESHAR:

DENG: Yes or no?

DESHAR:

DENG: You have to sign this and in your voice apologize for it.

DESHAR:

DENG: No one just goes and burns themselves. It's painful.

DESHAR:

DENG: So why would you? Did you get Independence? Did he come back? are you insane or idiotic? What is it?

DESHAR:

DENG: You can sign this and save lives. Do you get it? You can save thousands of lives by signing this! Tibetan, Han and Hui.

(DENG's alarm rings. DENG and LING sit in two chairs in the room facing each other taking a break. DENG immediately takes out his phone and checks.)

LIU: Can I go home tonight Inspector Deng?

DENG:

LIU: Inspector...any news of your daughter?

DENG: Is your family safe?

LIU: Yes.

DENG: Good.

LIU: Your daughter sir?

DENG: They wont hurt children.

LIU: No one knew they could hurt anyone sir.

DENG: We will burn theirs alive if they /

LIU: That's not what I am saying sir.

DENG: We don't hurt children.

LIU: Yes sir.

DENG: Savages. They are complete savages.

We are civilized.

LIU: Yes sir.

DENG: We work, for the country. We fight the West. We believe in equality. We are civilized.

LIU: Yes sir.

DENG: We will find Liu. *(DENG's alarm rings. They walk back to DESHAR. Splash water on her face. She wakes up.)*

DENG: The exact words, were in which dialect? Were they his words or translated? Who received it?

DESHAR:

DENG: You attacked me in your nunnery. I didn't even touch you. *(DESHAR folds her hands, in apology.)*

DENG: I should have had you arrested, then and there. I should have buried you in the rubble as well.

DENG: I won't ask you again. I need you to confess to who made you do it.

DESHAR:

DENG: I am not going to have my entire life destroyed because of some uneducated young nun's act of idiotic bravery. Is that clear? *(DESHAR is heard chanting under her breath.)*

DESHAR: *(In pain.)* Pah-la.

DENG *(Takes out his phone, shows DESHAR Liu's picture.)* Here... here...look at this. This is Liu my daughter.

(DESHAR tries to say her name feebly.)

DENG: Liu...I said Liu. *(Prays silently for her.)*

DENG: Don't pray for her. She is alive. *(DESHAR opens her eyes. Looks at him and prays again.)*

DENG: Stop it...I said. *(DESHAR continues to pray.)*

DENG: Stop it...I said...just stop it. *(DESHAR stops and opens her eyes.)*

DENG: Ling.

LING: Sir?

DENG: Separate her hands. Make her stop praying for my daughter.

LING: Sir?

DENG: Do it. *(LING tries to hold DESHAR's hand. Then her finger. Part of it, crumbles and falls. LING throws up. DESHAR screams. DENG's alarm rings. DENG begins to splash his face with water and LING sits in her chair holding herself from throwing up more. DESHAR in pain, sits and chants on her chair.)*

LING: It's cold...

DENG: Some fire can keep us warm.

LING: I need to go home sir.

DENG: Tomorrow. Tomorrow. Tomorrow.

LING: It's been 7 days.

DENG: And 7 nights.

LING: She is going to die.

DENG: Everyone should die. Everybody in these rooms.

LING: And everyone in this city who is not Tibetan, will fall under Tibetan swords and burn in this new Tibetan fire. *(Pause.)*

LING: I received a call, my dog was burnt. *(Pause.)*

LING: My brother sent a message, his legs were burnt. *(Pause.)*

LING: Someone burnt my old school teacher's school.

DENG *(Looking at his phone.)* 8 Tibetan children, burnt 3 Han children thrice. Burnt, poured water, dried them and burnt them again, not once not twice but thrice.

Ling: Sir, I want to go home.

DENG: Tomorrow. Tomorrow. Tomorrow.

LING: I have started throwing up at the sight of water.

DENG: You must drink water Ling. Water is essential to/

LING: Fire…there is so much fire…just so much fire… *(His alarm rings again.)*

(They come down. DENG pours petrol on DESHAR. Gives a matchbox to LING.)

DENG: I won't ask you again. I need you to confess to who made you do it.

DENG: Burn her.

LING: Sorry what…

DENG: Yes burn her. Again.

LING: Sir?

DENG: They are uncivilized savages…burn her. *(LING is frozen. DENG is looking at her. The phone rings.)*

DENG: Comrade…yes comrade… *(Closes his eyes.)* Yes comrade. Every cell is full. No Comrade, we can have more. They are after all criminals. For the motherland *(Keeps the phone.)*

(Pause.) 2 young Tibetan boys were trying to burn a pregnant Han woman. Raising slogans, that the Han should be burnt in their mother's womb.

It's, as if. you have given them a licence to burn.

This is your revolution. This is the non violence of His Holiness.

(DESHAR folds her hands. Is in tears. Praying.)

DENG: I'll make you speak. And the polygraph will not let you lie. *(DESHAR can be heard chanting feebly. Green light on polygraph.)*

SCENE 3

Later at night. In DESHAR's room.

DESHAR is lying down. LING walks in with medicines. Looks at the medicines that are lying next to her.

LING: Seven tablets, three ointments, and two bottles of saline…why are you not taking them *(DESHAR opens her eyes and looks at LING.*

LING: Here. This is what you have. *(Silence.)*

LING: Is the bed comfortable? *(DESHAR nods and continues to pray.)*

(LING takes out some pills and pours a glass of water. Walks up to DESHAR.)

LING: Open. *(DESHAR keeps her mouth shut.)*

LING: Open… *(DESHAR does not open her mouth.)*

LING: It will hurt if I force them down your throat. *(DESHAR looks at her. Shuts her eyes again and continues to pray.)*

LING: Ok… *(She takes the pills starts popping them into her mouth one by one. After two she drinks some water.)*

(DESHAR opens her eyes and looks at LING.)

(LING pops some more. Fills her mouth with pills.)

DESHAR: Don't *(LING is about to drink water.)*

DESHAR: *(Trying to be loud in a feeble voice.)* DON'T.

(LING puts the glass to her mouth, DESHAR moves her hand to snatch the glass away from LING's, the glass and her beads fall to the floor. DESHAR immediately bends to pick up the Beads and collapses on the floor.)

LING: Deshar! *(LING holds DESHAR's head in her hands.)*

(Silence.)

LING: Up…get up. *(DESHAR tries to get up holding LING. LING tries to lift her but fails. DESHAR is unstable and falls again.)*

(LING sits down exhausted on the floor and DESHAR takes her beads and continues to count beads and pray.)

LING: I am bad with suffering. *(DESHAR looks at her.)*

LING: I said, I am bad with suffering.

DESHAR: Those pills… can kill you.

LING: Someone has to take them. They need to be consumed.

DESHAR: I won't.

LING: Then I will.

DESHAR: I can't have your murder on my head.

LING: And I can't have yours.

DESHAR: You are a prison guard.

LING: You…a criminal.

DESHAR: I caused no harm to anyone.

LING: You can speak. More than a few words.

DESHAR: I didn't burn my tongue.

LING: You have been silent through the interrogation.

DESHAR: I have nothing to say. *(Silence.)*

LING: People are burning others in your name.

DESHAR: I don't know why.

LING: You did it.

DESHAR: I...I burnt on a railway track. Alone. On a mountain.

LING: They believe you are his message. *(DESHAR remains quiet.)*

(LING slowly goes towards DESHAR, tries to lift her again.)

(DESHAR gets up with great effort and sits on the bed.)

LING: I have been on duty for a week. Day and night. Please don't make this difficult.

DESHAR: I don't want to heal.

LING: I can kill you. You know that.

DESHAR: Yes.

LING: But you want to die. *(DESHAR remains quiet.)*

(LING starts to take out medicines from the box again.)

LING: It's the new world order. Criminals who want to die. The ultimate challenge of law and order. How do you punish those with a death wish.

Here...open your mouth. I promise I will have to take all the pills otherwise. Right here in front of your eyes.

DESHAR: Let me die.

LING: In just this week, there have been 18 arrests just in the women's cell for self immolation, and 8 we couldn't even save. You...you are responsible for all this. *(Silence.)* *(DESHAR closes her eyes.)*

LING: I am exhausted…I haven't slept, haven't gone home, haven't seen my family…in a week. The motherland does not pay me to take care of mercenaries like yourself.

DESHAR: Mercenaries?

LING: You really want me to believe, that out of the blue, a month after your nunnery was broken, that too to build a hospital, one day you suddenly realized the plight of the Tibetan people and burnt yourself?

DESHAR: I burnt long ago. In my mind. In the mind, is where it matters. *(Pause.)* And the re-education. What is that? What kind of education, derobes one's teachers, insults one's companions, destroys places of education…I had no other choice.

LING: And now you feel like talking? *(Silence.)*

DESHAR: In the interrogation, he was not talking. He was threatening. I am not afraid of threats. I am talking because you are. *(LING takes out an ointment and gently applies it on DESHAR's legs. DESHAR does not move. They look at each other.)*

DESHAR: You are struggling.

LING: What do you want?

DESHAR: What do you want?

LING: I don't want anything. Just heal and go. Get out. If you heal, this insanity will stop.

DESHAR: You don't like the sight of burnt people. *(LING gets up and looks at DESHAR in surprise.)*

LING: I am touching your wounds nun Deshar. Don't dismiss the benevolence of the ordinary. You did this for a little money, or name, but I do it for the love of the motherland. Put yourself in my shoes. Three nuns died on the chair today. In front of my eyes. Just out of burns. You think this is easy? Is it easy for us? *(Silence. She applies the ointment again.)*

DESHAR: I don't understand.

LING: What.

DESHAR: How do you know, they are burning in my name.

LING: They are carrying pictures.

DESHAR: Of?

LING: Yours and the Dalai Lama's *(Silence.)*

DESHAR: Buddhism forbids/

LING: Doesn't Buddhism forbid killing oneself? *(DESHAR is silent.)*

DESHAR: You are pure.

LING: Everyone is pure. People don't need to burn themselves to prove it.

DESHAR: I did not do it on anyone's instructions. *(LING remains quite. Keeps applying the ointment and dressing her wounds. DESHAR keeps looking at her.)*

DESHAR:I did not receive any orders from His Holiness' office or the monastery. I just lit up. I did not burn. And everyone else is becoming this light, in these times of darkness. *(Silence.)*

DESHAR: Constable Ling…I promise, on the Buddha. I did not/ *(LING is about to slap DESHAR but stops herself. Hits the wheel chair instead. DESHAR screams.)*

LING: Couldn't you have said this in the bloody interrogation room. The Polygraph would have recorded it. We could have saved you.

They are bringing in nun after nun to the chair because you are sitting there, busy playing god and peace manifest! Who the hell do you people think you are?

DESHAR: My denial would not mean a thing.

LING: How do you know? Are we maniacs? We interrogate 800 people every year…do you realize 800 at least on that chair. We need to change the chair every month, because it breaks! Do you believe we cannot tell when someone is telling the truth and when someone is not?

DESHAR: Clearly you cannot read a silence.

LING: No we cannot. We cannot read silence because interrogation reports do not say, the subject was silent, which could mean the subject is playing fucking god… thank you very much.

You people. Your smug bloody attitude. You should be shot dead. Just shot dead.

DESHAR: You are angry.

LING: Yes I am…I am angry because you have killed 3 nuns today as much as I have. And you better get angry too. Or sad or happy or something…"its playing in mind…in my mind" I believe. We are building, roads and trains, and you are sitting in bloody government funded monasteries, discussing the nature of truth and now getting on the roads and burning yourselves because truth is playing in your bloody minds. *(Silence. LING goes back to applying the ointment on DESHAR's wounds.)*

DESHAR: I burnt my body, to present my mind. There was no other way.

LING: I can't change your mind. Have the pills. heal your body.

DESHAR: Let me die. I will pray that it heals your mind.

LING: Deshar, I don't know what will happen to you and me. But I have a cousin who lives with us. 8 years old. He is Han, but has Tibetan friends. He does not recognize himself as Han or them as Tibetans. Last night, he came to my office to give me food that my mother had cooked for me. He saw me and started to cry. For the first time he asked me, do Tibetans burn Sister? I was born in Tibet Sister, am I Tibetan,will I have to burn too?

I don't know what your god has told you Nun Deshar, but I do not have a god but my common sense tells me, that we should leave a world for our children with some decent choices. And I don't think to burn oneself can be one of them...

DESHAR: Our children have no choices. My father fought against all the odds to raise me by himself.

LING: Your Pah-la, has been arrested today. He is in the prison next door. *(Silence.)*

DESHAR: I don't mean anything to him. Let him go.

LING: You are upset about your father, about your god, about your land. Nun Deshar, life is not always understood by meditating on it. Sometimes it's just important to engage with it. To fight it out.

DESHAR: Why are you doing this?

LING: Maybe because my mind burns too. But I do not have the luxury of a set of beads. *(Silence.)*

LING: Are you going to take the pills.

DESHAR: Is it going to make you less angry? *(LING gives DESHAR the pills.)*

DESHAR: If I die, will it stop?

LING: What?

DESHAR: The Violence.

LING: If you tell the truth, it will. *(Pause.)*

DESHAR: The Truth. To a machine that believes, silence is
a lie.

LING: Every god has his rules. Yours believes, the truth, is
fire. Mine, that falsity, a beep.

DESHAR: I will speak.

LING: Here. *(DESHAR takes the medicines.)*

DESHAR: Have you seen him?

LING: Whom?

DESHAR: Pah-la.

LING: Every father whose daughter is in a prison cell,
looks the same. I might have. But I can't tell. I can't tell
anymore.

SCENE 4

*Inspector DENG's office. TSERING is standing next to a chair.
CONSTABLE GAPHEL is in the room.*

GAPHEL: Water?

TSERING: *(Looks at him in surprise.)* Hospitality? *(GAPHEL puts
some water in front of TSERING.)*

GAPHEL: Are you ok commander?

TSERING: Beads?

GAPHEL: I am Buddhist.

   (Pause.) Gaphel?

(Pause. TSERING looks at GAPHEL carefully.)

GAPHEL: I was with you Commander Tsering, don't you recognize me? *(Pause.)*

GAPHEL: *(Even more cautiously.)* I am Gaphel...you remember we trained in Colorado together? And we were air dropped together. *(Pause.)* As in we were going to be, you jumped and I did not.

TSERING: Why didn't you jump?

GAPHEL: *(Silence.)* I was afraid. I did not have the courage to jump from the airplane in the end. *(Pause.)*

TSERING: Why have I been arrested?

GAPHEL: Your daughter.

TSERING: She's dead. *(Pause.)* I heard she burnt herself?

GAPHEL: Yes.

TSERING: So?.

GAPHEL: For interrogation.

TSERING: I have not seen her in years. Ever since she became a nun.

GAPHEL: We want to ask some basic questions.

TSERING: Like?

GAPHEL: The truth.

TSERING: The truth? *(Pause.)*

GAPHEL: About who made her do this.

TSERING: You. Or him. *(Pointing at a portrait of Mao Tse Tung.)*

(Pause.)

TSERING: I do not know anything. Whatever your name is. May I go now?

I have students waiting.

GAPHEL: I am here to help commander.

TSERING: What?

GAPHEL: What do you teach?

TSERING: The truth. *(Beat.)*

GAPHEL: I meant which subject?

TSERING: Tibetan.

GAPHEL: Where.

TSERING: In a school. I run from home.

GAPHEL: Commander, I tried to reach you. You weren't there.

TSERING:When?

GAPHEL: I came with the unit.

TSERING: Now?

GAPHEL: For…re-education.

TSERING: On the train, I presume? *(Pause.)*

GAPHEL: Yes.

TSERING: You burnt her. *(Pause, TSERING drinks water.)*

GAPHEL: Your daughter's…burning…has caused riots in Lhasa.

TSERING: Riots? I wouldn't know. I live in my province.

GAPHEL: If you answer my questions, I can get you out of here sooner commander. *(Pause.)* In your province, five others have self-immolated.

TSERING: Is that the new name for It? Good. I wouldn't know, I don't go out much.

GAPHEL: You do realize commander that she started it?

TSERING: Oh…that's generous. I thought Mao Tse Tung did.

GAPHEL: Do you know if she received orders from anyone.

TSERING: I don't.

GAPHEL: Didn't she meet you one last time…before/

TSERING: I don't meet nuns and monks. No matter who they are.

GAPHEL: So you are not a practicing Buddhist?

TSERING: I am the only one. *(Pause.)*

GAPHEL: Commander…do you realize that this is a big crime? Treason? They won't let you go easily. You must cooperate.

TSERING: They? Who's they? And why are you calling me commander. What am I commanding?

GAPHEL: I am Gaphel, commander. Your fellow soldier. You don't recognize me?

TSERING: I do not recognize you. I do not recognize, the Chinese, state, the Chinese army, the Chinese government, Chinese products, Chinese flag, Chinese Olympics but most of all I do not recognize Tibetans who did not jump.

(Long pause. TSERING stares at GAPHEL.)

GAPHEL: This won't help.

TSERING: What?

GAPHEL: I am trying to help you. You need to cooperate.

TSERING: For what?

GAPHEL: To be free.

TSERING: Free. If I cooperate, we will be free? Fine, I'll cooperate. Please let me know when is this freedom due though.

GAPHEL: I meant leave the prison?

TSERING: Oh…that. You call that, walking around and shopping and visiting Nangma bars freedom. That one.

GAPHEL: Your daughter gave her life Commander for/

TSERING: I don't care about what monks and nuns do. Is that clear?

GAPHEL: If you tell us what we need to know.

TSERING: I don't understand. What do you want me to tell you.

GAPHEL: We want you to tell us If she received orders from…
(Silence.)

(TSERING looks at him.)

(GAPHEL looks around. Takes out a picture of The Dalai Lama from an inner pocket in his coat and shows it to TSERING.)

TSERING: *(Laughs.)* You are afraid to say his name in your own office.

GAPHEL: We turned non violent when he ordered commander. The party wants to know if this time he has ordered the violence.

TSERING: Violence.

His Holiness. Is my god. I do not agree with him on
everything, but he is my god. I wish he had ordered
violence against all of you, but unfortunately I don't think
he has.

GAPHEL: Unfortunately?

You are a Buddhist, and the Buddha proposed a middle
path. And so does his holiness. The middle path is your
Dharma...your way of life/

TSERING: Middle path it is. Here I am, the ordinary Tibetan,
bang in the middle of the god of compassion and the god
of land rights...the Monk and the Marxist *(Looking at the
picture or Dalai Lama and Mao.)*, bang in the middle of
two absolutely genuine, well meaning, peaceful people,
wanting to liberate me!.

GAPHEL: He is our god, he can see the future.

TSERING: If he could see the future, he should not have
allowed his own brother to form a guerrilla army and for it
to be out there in Nepal, in Mustang fighting the Chinese
and then call the movement off one day, abruptly. I saw
the commanders shoot themselves in front of me in the
room you idiot, there was no way of returning. Even
Chairman Mao never abandoned his soldiers like this.

(Pause.)

But you wouldn't know. You are a deserter and now you
work for the enemy. Welcome to Tibet!

GAPHEL: You, do not really believe commander Tsering
that the guerillas could have won over the Chinese in the
guerilla war, do you? A few men trained in Colorado by
the CIA, form an army of Khampas, a nomadic tribe for

all practical purposes, and take on the People's liberation Army. What are the chances, that we would have won?

TSERING: And now...have we won? With our Lamas leading our political thought, have we found what we were looking for?

GAPHEL: We have the Tibetan Government in Exile, commander. With his holiness leading us, you have the Tibetan culture intact.

TSERING: Culture...of course. Living in similar looking settlements in mini mountains all over the world, we have culture! We have culture, between an AIDS epidemic in our settlments and rising cases of drug abuse amongst the young.

Between selling momos on the streets of New York and prayer flags in the markets of New Delhi.

We have culture because our children watch Tibetan dance and turn the odd prayer wheel, thrice a year at their local non profit's fundraiser. We have culture because His Holiness is the next most popular face on cotton T shirts, only after Che Guevera! Culture!

GAPHEL: I am talking about the government in /

TSERING: And of course we have the government in EXILE. What does that even mean, the government in exile?

GAPHEL: It means, when we get our land back, we will already have a democratic way of life in place. A fool proof plan for the future.

TSERING: So we have decided the colour of the walls of the imaginary house that we are going to build, on a patch of land that we do not own. The shape and size of the parliament, mind you is all in place. Rejoice Tibetans, your Holiness has given you blue prints for science

67

fiction. You have many lives, This time, placate yourself with the nobel prize, and after three lives, if you are still unfortunate enough to be Tibetan, come back for your democracy.

GAPHEL: Commander Tsering, his Holiness has held our entire community together.

Just look at what you have done to yourself.

TSERING: I have not done this to myself...the two of you have. My people who did not jump and my god who did not stay.

GAPHEL: Commander, your god did not stay, in order to save the struggle. If he was here, there would be no Tibetan struggle to speak of.

(Pause.)

GAPHEL: We have to stop this new violence commander?

TSERING: I didn't start anything. I am not going to stop anyone *(Pause.)* Who knows, finally we might have an uprising.

GAPHEL: Uprisings don't have loot, rape and arson Commander. 1959 was an uprising.

If we call this an uprising, we will belittle our movement.

TSERING: You want a revolution, but you want chants to beat atomic bombs and automatic machine guns. You want candle marches under police protection and pretty boys and girls singing We Shall Overcome in every other language, than Tibetan. *(Mockingly.)* Our Movement.

The communists can only be defeated by the Americans, and that was our only real chance.

GAPHEL: The Americans are nobody's. They are loyal to none.

TSERING: They were loyal to us you bastard.

GAPHEL: You are wrong commander. Absolutely wrong.

His Holiness was the voice on the tape but Nixon called the movement off.

He was to visit China. They pulled the plug on our movement.

If His Holiness had not sent the tapes, you would have all been butchered in some Nepalese hill town, bordered by the Chinese, and that too with no food, water or guns.

(Pause.)

TSERING: Nixon?

GAPHEL: There isn't a movement in this world Commander Tsering, that the Americans have not betrayed. You know everything about the movement in exile, you don't know who called your movement off!

The Americans.

(Laughs.)

You think the Americans care about our democracy and our Dalai Lama. They don't give a damn. I harbour no illusions about them and their support. Violent or non violent.

They like robes and prayer beads and they like to occupy Wall Street a little less than they like their basketball… Their film stars do Buddhism in private retreats with security guards at the doors. They sell dumplings in the streets of New York and San Francisco with an imaginary snow lion flag on weekends, to relieve themselves of their

69

moral burden of being the blood suckers of the world.
I am not relying on the Americans for our movement
Commander. I am however, relying on our children in
Exile.

The Americans are imperialists Monday to Friday. On
Saturday they want to save the world and on Sunday they
go to church.

You want liberation…true liberation….look for oil in
Tibet. You will have American warships in our lakes. Only
till they get everything they want.

You want your young to die, ask the Americans to support
your guerrilla movement.

They will sell a whole lot of guns and then go back to
baseball, as we kill our young.

*(DENG walks in. GAPHEL is startled. Quickly puts the picture
away. Salutes.)*

(DENG looks at TSERING. He remains seated.)

DENG: *(To GAPHEL.)* Is there a problem constable?

GAPHEL: No…no sir.

DENG: Is he an old…friend or…

GAPHEL: No…no sir.

DENG: I am inspector Deng. Head. On deputation. Is that
clear? Did he answer?

GAPHEL: No Commander. Give me some time. I will…
I promise.

(DENG shows his hand to him. He stops.)

DENG: What's with your daughter?

(TSERING remains quite.)

DENG: She didn't meet you before burning? *(Pause.)*

No. I know you were a shit soldier from your files, are you a shit father as well?

(TSERING remains quite.)

DENG: I saw her. *(Pause.)*

DENG: Yes. And while she was being asked questions, she said Pah-la...Pah-la...that's why we got you.

TSERING: You interrogated her?

DENG: On life support. We want the truth.

TSERING: You killed her!

DENG: No. *(Silence.)*

TSERING: *(Now almost in tears.)* Where is she? *(DENG takes out his phone. Shows him a picture.)*

DENG: Is this her? *(TSERING lets out a scream of horror. He is now in tears.)*

TSERING: Deshar...

DENG: Now can we stop being smart and get on with what you know.

TSERING: I want to see her...please...I want to *(DENG shows him another picture. TSERING looks at it and looks at him.)*

DENG: That's my daughter. Liu. 8 years old. Missing for a week! I want to see her you asshole. *(Silence.)*

DENG: Put him in the cell. Tomorrow morning, I want him in the room. *(Goes close to TSERING.)*

Pray...pray that I find my daughter. Pray.

SCENE 5

Late Night. JIA is in the playground of her daughter's school. School bags, lunch boxes, water bottles are strewn around. Ribbons of little girls have fallen. Some of them are still tied to chunks of hair.

A man with a stick is rummaging through it. He is picking up hair and putting it in a plastic bag.

MAN: Your girl?

JIA: Yes.

MAN: Do you see that truck? It dropped them somewhere and came back.

JIA: Some?

MAN: Yes. Some. Others…you can see can't you?

JIA: My daughter runs quite fast.

MAN: Faster than the others I hope.

JIA: This? Here…this one…

MAN: What is it?

JIA: It's her water bottle.

MAN: Are you sure?

JIA: Yes.

MAN: Has a boy's name on it.

JIA: Where.

MAN: Here, at the back.

JIA: Oh…yes.

MAN: I hope you do not find any of her belongings here.

JIA: Why?

MAN: Would mean she was not in danger isn't it?.

JIA: True.

MAN: So?

JIA: Isn't there another way.

MAN: You want to know where the truck took them don't you?

JIA: Yes.

MAN: So I could tell you. No one else could.

JIA: I know.

MAN: So...go for it.

JIA: I am married.

MAN: I don't want to marry you.

JIA: Can I give you a...hand job. Or a blow job or something.

MAN: Mmm...what if I just told you that they are in Lhasa. Or say in southern Lhasa. Will that help?

JIA: Aren't you Buddhist?

MAN: Oh yes...here. *(Shows her beads.)* That's why they spared me when they came back after a few days.

JIA: So what about.

MAN: Listen...i don't want a moral lesson right now. There's enough of that in my life. My mind's buzzing with the moral theories of an ascetic. This...look. This is real life. You fuck with us, we fuck back with you.

JIA: But.

MAN: Listen…there's no pressure. A lot of mothers are willing. You can leave.

(Looks at her.) It's not even like you are, you know…it's all very…loose…and you know…so…so Chinese in a way. *(Laughs out.)*

JIA: Ok…so where.

MAN: Here…here.

JIA: In the middle of this.

MAN: Yes. Where else. It's safe. No one comes in to the school anymore after that day. It's safe.

Make some space…get ready. I'll see if I can find anything and I'll come.

JIA: Ok *(JIA undresses. Lies down next to a set of lunch boxes, water bottles and some hair. She waits for him.)*

JIA: I am ready.

MAN: Do you have…some…lipstick maybe? *(JIA takes out her lipstick. Applies it. Throws it away.)*

MAN: How will you go back.

JIA: The way I came.

MAN: Is it quieter now?

JIA: In some parts of the city.

MAN: Then.

JIA: I am a policeman's wife. I have a card so/

MAN: A policeman's wife did you say?

JIA: Yes.

MAN: I have never slept with a policeman's wife. That and
    the lipstick. It's something.

JIA: Listen let's do this quickly. I want to find my girl.

MAN: That place where I have taken them, is quite safe. Good
    food and everything. Nice people.

JIA: Where is it.

MAN: Spread your legs. *(JIA does so.)*

MAN: Moan. Just a little it turns me on. I am quite old you
    see. Becomes difficult. *(JIA…looks at him in disbelief.)*

JIA: You want me to moan?

MAN: Yes…yes…that would be nice. If you moan now,
    eventually it will be easier for you.

JIA: This is violence.

MAN: I know. I know.

JIA: Can you keep your beads away at least.

MAN: Oh why. How does it matter to you?

JIA: I am feeling more for them than you are clearly.

MAN: I am chanting. I am in. Not a moment when I do
    not remind myself to keep calm, love everyone, take
    responsibility for my actions and all that. Moan come on.
    (JIA moans.)

    *(The man collects some more hair in his plastic bag. Walks down
    to JIA. Takes off his pants is about to get into her when JIA spots
    something and moves away. The man falls.)*

JIA: Oh…oh…Liu…

MAN: Easy…you'll kill me.

JIA: This is…her diary. See it has her name.

MAN: Oh…let me see.

JIA: I know it…here…this is my writing. A night before I wrote a note to her teacher and/

MAN: Oh…that's not good then.

JIA: What.

MAN: If you get the diary.

JIA: Why?

MAN: It means her bag was opened. As in there was time…I have to give you the other address now.

JIA: What other address.

MAN: Where those who were killed were dumped.

JIA: What!

MAN: What else do you think everyone was running from?

JIA: Why on earth would Buddhists kill children?

MAN: Why on earth would someone remain Buddhist in this country.

JIA: No…that's not…she must have dropped this. While running or playing.

Give me the address of the place where they are alive. Please.

MAN: Ok…you don't want the address of the place where the dead are.

JIA: No…no she's alive…

MAN: Fine…come…lie down. *(JIA lies down. Moans. The man goes close to her. Stops. Sits next to her.)*

(Silence.)

MAN: You want to know, why are we suddenly violent?

JIA: No. I want the address.

MAN: If we suddenly turned non violent, you would have liked to know.

JIA:

MAN: You have made violence normal. You are only surprised that it's against you.

JIA: I have never hurt anyone.

MAN: I know. I know. I am saying you. I need a face to accuse. I have to live. *(Pause.)*

MAN: I try but I can't do it you know… *(Laughs.)* Should I write it in the diary.

JIA: Yes… *(The man writes the address.)*

MAN: Half an hour. Take the back lanes *(JIA walks away with the diary. Stops and comes back.)*

JIA: What's the other address?

MAN: Sorry?

JIA: The other address.

MAN: Ok…I'll give it to you for a blow job. That should work. *(Pause.)* Just for you.

JIA: Ok.

MAN: It will take me a little time though. I don't want to do this with anger.

JIA: Yes sure.

MAN: You want to look for her things. Ten-fifteen minutes I promise. Won't be long.

JIA: Ok. *(She sits down disgusted with herself, holding on to the diary.)*

MAN: I came here 2 weeks ago. You are coming too late.

JIA: Don't you work here?

MAN: No.

JIA: Then.

MAN: My daughter was in this school too.

My only daughter. My wife is not with us anymore, so she was all I had.

JIA: I thought you are Tibetan.

MAN: Yes. As Tibetan as it gets.

JIA: And?

MAN: I saved those I could. Some girls who were hiding. Burnt or buried the rest. I did my part. Service. I am a Buddhist.

JIA: Your daughter?

MAN: I have found some of her hair. She had beautiful hair. It's in the bag *(They are quiet.)*

MAN: Come...I am ready. Can you use some more lipstick please? *(He picks it up and offers it.)*

JIA: Sure... *(JIA goes closer. Takes it from him and applies it. Gets on her knees in front of him. The man keeps looking at the packet of hair. JIA at the diary in her hand.)*

SCENE 6

(Next night. The roof of the prison. Its snowing. Flashlights everywhere. DENG is on his knees, looking at his daughter's photograph, mirroring JIA's posture at the end of the last scene but not at the same place. Enter LING.)

(LING comes close to him and stands. Holds him. He holds her and resists his desire to cry out aloud. LING comforts him.)

DENG: Her mother called.

LING:

DENG: They burnt her. In the name of the Dalai Lama, in the name of the Buddha, they…

LING: I am…sorry.

DENG: It must have been so painful…so…so painful. My…

LING: You should go home inspector Deng.

DENG: For what?

LING: To be with your wife.

DENG: She called. She won't be there.

LING: You have to mourn her death.

DENG: I am a father Ling. I held her first.

LING: Yes.

DENG: I am a father, I stayed up all night, if she had a cough.

LING: Yes.

DENG: I made mistakes while playing her games, so that she would correct me. I fed her, clothed her, bathed her and I always made a deliberate little mistake in every step, so

79

that she would correct me and I would applaud her for who she was.

LING: Yes inspector Deng...

DENG: I am a father. I loved her, just her, more than I loved to hate the brutality of this world. I loved her more than I loved to grow up myself and realize what a mess I had been handed to save. This world, this world, it can have no more fathers, if I am not a father.

I am a father Ling. There will be no Tibetan fathers here on. Their children will burn in this prison one by one. I am not going anywhere Ling...I am a father, I will avenge her death.

(LING looks at him in silence.)

(LING walks away.)

DENG: I don't care about the party Ling. I will kill that nun and her father together. Make him watch his daughter's death. I'll burn her in front of /

LING: You didn't look for her. *(Pause.)*

DENG: What?

LING: You didn't look for her, Inspector Deng. You didn't even look for Liu.

DENG: I was here. With you. For the motherland. *(Pause.)*

LING: You were saving yourself. *(Silence.)*

DENG: Have you lost your mind?

LING:

DENG: I have lost a child. Do you know what that means?

LING: My deepest condolences.

DENG: I am a father. He is a father. He should watch his child die. She wanted to burn. Mine didn't.

LING: That is the problem Inspector Deng.

DENG: What is the problem?

LING: You're a father. He's a father *(Pause.)*

LING: Mao tse tung…a father, Shakyamuni Buddha… a father, *(In a mocking tone.)* His Holiness the Dalai Lama is a father…Stalin, Lenin, Khruschev were fathers. Nixon, Regan, Bush are fathers. Xi Jinping is a father, Hu Jintao was a father…and fathers are not just fathers of a child,but fathers of the nation, of an idea, of the people. That is the problem. Fathers.

DENG: You are insane.

LING: My father on his deathbed, asked for forgiveness from his dead father's portrait, while my mother worked in a brick factory to bring home our dinner that night. *(Silence.)*

LING: Nun Deshar, burns herself to protest without hurting anyone else at all, and you fathers are burning each other's children night and day.

The world doesn't need less monasteries or Marxists, Inspector Deng. It needs less fathers.

DENG: You are crossing your line.

(LING turns around and begins to leave.)

DENG: Ling…Ling!! *(She turns around.)*

DENG: Ling, comfort me.

LING: No… *(DENG looks at her surprised.)*

LING: I owe it to your daughter. That you are not comforted. None of you.

DENG: I will die Ling…I will die…please please comfort me. *(LING walks back to him.)*

DENG: Comfort me Ling…comfort me. *(Desperately holds her.)*

LING *(Takes out DENG's gun from his holster and gives it to him.)* Here…shoot me *(DENG looks at her in shock.)*

LING: Shoot me. Nothing else will give you comfort. Blood for blood. Just shoot me, or anyone else you mildly care about and see how comforted you feel.

DENG: I am not the monster tonight. *(Silence.)*

DENG: I am not the monster. comfort me.

LING: Shoot me. but I won't comfort you Deng.

DENG: You built a home on government money. You cannot leave this job in 10 years.

LING: Yes.

DENG: If you lose your job though, all of you will be on the streets.

LING: You are pathetic Deng.

DENG: Comfort me. I don't have anyone else here.

LING: You want sex?

DENG: No.

LING: A mother.

DENG: Yes.

LING: *(Laughs.)* The limits of complexity of the masculine mind. Sex or motherhood. Basic. Basic simple shit.

DENG: Don't mock me Ling. Comfort me.

LING: You want me to hold you and let you cry.

DENG: Yes perhaps.

LING: And if I refuse?

DENG: I will fire you from the job right away. I am not asking for much. I am not the monster tonight.

LING *(Laughs.)* My father used to scare me when I did not love him.

DENG: A human being can ask for solace, the night his daughter is killed.

LING *(Laughs.)* My father cried when I called him out in my teens. He cried and made me cry till I comforted him for being guilty of being nasty to me.

DENG: I am not your father.

LING: I am not your child.

DENG: I am your superior.

LING: I do not have to comfort you.

DENG: I am a human being. I deserve empathy.

LING: *(Laughs.)* There is a communist hell, where fathers rot and read popular female fiction.

DENG: I'll fire you Ling. You'll die in poverty.

LING: Do it. I won't comfort you.

DENG: You don't understand. You will have no choice. No other job, no other/

LING: Do it...do it. I owe it to your daughter.

DENG: You are heartless.

LING *(Laughing.)* I think I have started a revolution.

DENG: Which is?

LING: Don't comfort the fathers. Let them die in guilt.

DENG: You may leave. I can cope with this alone. *(Silence. LING is standing and smiling.)*

DENG: You may leave, I will /

LING: You don't want sex, and you won't get my motherhood. Now there is only one thing that you can do *(DENG looks at her.)*

LING: Resort to mindless violence. *(Pause.)* That is the gift our fathers have given us in the last one hundred years.

DENG: I only want the truth.

LING: In the name of truth, love and security for their children.

DENG: You should resign. If I fire you, it will be worse.

LING: Fire me. I won't resign *(Pause.)*

DENG: Who killed my daughter?

LING *(Laughs.)* All of you fathers. The shape of the world.

DENG: The party wants the truth. I want these Buddhists to feel what I feel.

LING: You will interrogate them to death, when you do not care about the answer.

DENG: I am not the monster Ling.

LING: No you are not.

DENG: I represent the people's worker.

LING: No.

DENG: I represent the only people who stood up to the west.

LING: No.

DENG: I/

LING: You represent testosterone. You are a gland, not an ideology.

I am going. Fire me.

DENG: You are responsible for what will happen to your family from here on *(LING smiles.)*

LING: Do you know what the Dalai Lama has said.

DENG: You cannot take his name.

LING: The next Dalai Lama is a woman.

DENG: The beginning of the end.

LING: *(Laughs.)* He won the Nobel prize. He is being progressive!

DENG: He wants headlines.

LING: Can you imagine a woman heading the party in the next 100 years!

DENG: We are not weak.

LING *(Laughs.)* You don't understand.

DENG: What.

LING: I am not sure how reincarnation works, but if only women can reincarnate as women, you might actually help him out by killing the nun.

DENG: That's bullshit.

LING: That is if your daughter has not reincarnated as the next Dalai Lama already *(Laughs.)* Do you think children of marxists can reincarnate as Buddhist Nuns?.

Can you imagine, you...you Inspector Deng, in charge of Lhasa Prisons with an active part in the future of Tibet. You might be making the next Dalai Lama.

DENG: I do not believe in reincarnation.

LING: No. You don't believe in women. None of you do. This world is fathers fighting fathers. And hoping some of you will reincarnate across the line. *(Pause.)*

DENG: Get her to the polygraph room. Then you can leave.

LING: She is ready to die. I am ready to leave. It's just you two fathers. As always. This violence. It's just you.

DENG: You're fired. *(Pause.)*

LING: Gladly. Long live the revolution.

SCENE 7

Polygraph room. Dimly lit.

The machines are connected on DESHAR. TSERING is sitting in front of her. He has just entered. LING stands behind DESHAR. DESHAR has a butter lamp in her hands.

Silence as TSERING looks at DESHAR. DESHAR smiles.

TSERING: Get alright and we will go home in 3 days. Ok? *(All of them laugh.)*

TSERING: Ok...just get alright.

DESHAR: How are you, Pah-la?

TSERING: Good. Healthy. Next door. Thank god for 'the system' else we could not have met *(the three of them laugh.)*

DESHAR: Meet Ling... *(Pause.)*

DESHAR: She is a Buddha of the highest order.
A revolutionary. *(DESHAR Smiles.)*

(TSERING looks at LING. Folds his hand in gratitude. LING looks at him. Pause.)

DESHAR: It was my decision to burn Pah-la.

TSERING *(Looking away.)* Your anger Deshar, was with them.
Why did you/

DESHAR: I burnt of impermanance Pah-la. Not hatred.

(Pause.)

(She gives him the butter lamp. TSERING looks at her curiously and holds it. TSERING looks at her.)

DESHAR: Hold this.

This is Amala. Tell her you love her. *(TSERING keeps it back.)*

DESHAR: Look, she is dying, on a winter night, in the middle of snow. Right in front of the Buddha statue in our house, she is dying in your arms.

(TSERING looks at DESHAR. Picks up the butter lamp.)

(Pause.)

TSERING: Do you know what she said to me in the end?

DESHAR: No.

TSERING: I went to see his holiness, not because I didn't believe in your revolution. But because I want to save Deshar from hatred.

DESHAR: And you did. I have no hatred. You loved me and and left no room in me for anything else.

87

TSERING: *(Still looking at the butter lamp.)* Live. Please live. We saved our child. Look. *(Pause.)*

She bled to death on this arm. On the other arm, you slept. We had to save your life Deshar.

(Pause.)

Suicide is not revolution, Deshar.

DESHAR: Suicide is to hurt oneself, I was giving myself more life than I ever had before.

TSERING: When we were young /

DESHAR: You have had your revolution Pah-la. We are going to have ours.

(Pause.)

TSERING: By burning yourself?

DESHAR: I had to burn to make our voice heard. What the voice found, is the revolution.

(Pause.)

TSERING: What did the voice find?

DESHAR: The ability to not quiver when burning. To not scream when shouted at. To not go quiet when silenced.

TSERING: Your voice. Will it save the world?

DESHAR: It will make the world worth saving.

(Pause.)

DESHAR: Your generation was fighting for Tibet, Pah-la. Mine is fighting for the conscience of the world.

(Silence.)

88

(DENG enters. GAPHEL behind him. He looks at LING. Signals her to leave. She bows in front of DESHAR, kisses her hands. Looks at DENG.)

LING: For the motherland comrade. Remember... For the motherland. *(Hands him her badge. Leaves.)*

(Harsh lights are switched on.)

DENG: The Truth. *(Pause.)*

Tonight. We...

(Pause.)

DENG *(Goes to DESHAR.)* My daughter Liu, is dead. Burnt by your people. *(DESHAR shuts her eyes and prays.)*

DESHAR: I am sorry Commander Deng. I am sorry for your loss. May that beautiful child not have suffered in the end.

DENG: You killed her.

DESHAR: If taking my life relieves you of your suffering, I am prepared.

DENG: Why did you burn yourself?

DESHAR: To find a way of making my voice heard without hurting another sentient being.

DENG: My daughter isn't a sentient being?

DESHAR: She is. We shouldn't turn violent.

DENG: You do not understand Liberation?

DESHAR: Your way out of suffering is to liberate the outside. You are liberating the outside, we the inside. Our ways do not have to be at war with each other.

DENG: Can you bring my child back?

DESHAR:

DENG: If there is a god, can you do it?

DESHAR: My god is the god of compassion.

DENG: Bring back my child. I will let you go.

DESHAR:

DENG: Pray for her to come back to life, I will stop the
killings in the interrogation room.

Give her life and I will/

DESHAR: If I could bring her to life, I wouldn't need you to
do anything for it Deng. Her death has made the world
poorer.

(DENG sits on the floor. Next to DESHAR's feet. DESHAR holds him.)

(Looks at DESHAR.)

DENG: Your people attacked another school.

DESHAR: There is no one, who is another person inspector
Deng. There is no one else but us.

DENG: Three Han children died. You are giving me
metaphysics?

DESHAR: The evil in this world is ours. Yours and mine.

DENG: They left a portrait of the Dalai Lama on the school
gate.

DESHAR: We are not the portraits we carry. If we were, we
wouldn't burn the school.

DENG: You are so full of empty wisdom. All of you should be
shot dead. *(DENG picks out his gun. Points at DESHAR.)*

(TSERING is in shock. GAPHEL immediately stops DENG.)

GAPHEL: Commander…commander, we cannot shoot her Commander. We are in the polygraph room, we have orders to not do anything without the test. If she tells the truth, she can go commander. We cannot/

DENG: So you are on their side now?

GAPHEL: I am on the side of the people commander.

DENG: The People. Fine. *(Pause.)*

DENG: Let's play a game. A Truth game. One of you, father or daughter, sits on the chair…and we turn the polygraph on. Except that you play for the other.

I will ask you two questions. Just two.

If you tell the truth and it does not beep, the person you play for can go.

If you lie, the blood of a traitor will be on your hands.

There is no place for bourgeois reactionaries in the people's republic.

Does that seem fair Constable Gaphel?

(GAPHEL remains quiet.)

(TSERING gets up and sits on the chair.)

DENG: We'll have the nun first on the chair.

(GAPHEL tentatively connects her to the controls.)

DENG: Two questions. One beep and you lose your father.

DESHAR: I am ready.

DENG: Are you responsible for the death of my daughter, Liu?

(Silence.)

Are you responsi/

GAPHEL: This isn't a polygraph question, commander. *(DENG gestures towards him to remain quiet.)*

DESHAR: We are all responsible for every injustice that happens in this world. In this 'Samsara', the cycle of /

DENG: I am asking you a yes or no question? I am not in your nunnery, you are in my prison. *(DESHAR remains quiet.)*

DENG: Are you responsible for the death of my daughter Liu or not?

DESHAR: Yes, I am *(The green light on the polygraph glows. Does not beep.)*

(DENG looks at TSERING.)

DENG: You are?

DESHAR: Everyone in this room is. *(Pause.)* I am sorry. *(She looks at the green light. DENG looks at it.)*

DENG: Did you receive orders from His Holiness the Dalai Lama from India to burn yourself? Directly or indirectly?

DESHAR: I did not. *(The green light glows. No beep.)*

DENG: You are free Tsering. You may leave.

TSERING: *(Goes close to the interrogation chair.)* Connect the wires to me. I am ready.

(Pause. DENG looks at him sternly.)

DENG: For what?

TSERING: To play your game.

DENG: The game is for prisoners. You are free.

TSERING: I wasn't when you started.

DENG: Yes but now you are. We don't have anyone to play for the nun. *(Silence.)*

You should know what it means to lose your child.

DESHAR: *(With her eyes shut.)* Don't hate him Pah-la…don't hate him. *(Pause.)*

GAPHEL: You cannot do this commander. The party does not allow you, to change the rules!

DENG: THE PARTY DID NOT ALLOW ME TO SAVE MY CHILD! THE PARTY CANNOT FORCE ME TO SAVE THEIRS.

GAPHEL: You are a Marxist commander. You cannot/

(TSERING takes GAPHEL's gun and points at DENG. Immediately DENG draws his gun and points back.)

GAPHEL: Commander. *(To TSERING.)* Keep your gun down commander. Commander please.

TSERING: She hasn't lied, Deng. Not even once. You have no case. Let her go.

DENG: Shoot.

(Silence.)

(DENG lowers his gun slightly.)

DENG: Shoot.

DESHAR: Pah-la, please put your gun/

TSERING: I won't miss.

DENG: I know. Shoot.

GAPHEL: Keep your gun down commander. *(To DENG.)* He won't.

93

TSERING: I am sorry for the death of your child, Deng. If I were there, I would have given up my life to protect her.

DENG: You and I are violent men, Tsering

TSERING: We have let our children down already. Now let her go.

DENG: We are both bad fathers. In this world, fathers should not be ideological.

TSERING: My daughter is the last of her kind, Deng. A revolutionary who does not hate the oppressor. Without her, what world will you leave for your children?

DENG: I don't have my child. I have no world to leave for anyone.

TSERING: Revenge is not revolution, Deng.

DENG: Revenge is not revolution. Write that as the epitaph of my daughter's murderers.

TSERING: You cannot leave me out in the world and kill my daughter here, Deng. You cannot give me that freedom!

(TSERING moves forward to attack him without shooting. DENG holds him. A moment of silence. DENG shoots. DESHAR screams. GAPHEL closes his eyes. TSERING falls.)

(Silence.)

GAPHEL: *(Takes out his badge, throws it on the floor in front of DENG. Sits on the chair.)* I, I will play for the nun. Ask.

(Pause.)

DENG: I'll play for the nun, Gaphel. You take your commander out of this hell.

(Pause.)

DENG: I'll play.

(GAPHEL gets up, goes to TSERING's body, holds him tightly and cries sitting down.)

(DENG sits at the chair)

DENG: We cannot escape the system.

DESHAR: We will all be free, Deng. What will become of you?

DENG: Help me. Bring back my...

DESHAR: If my death gives you comfort, I am ready.

DENG: I'll play for you. Like your father would. *(Pause.)* You ask.

I will tell the truth. I promise.

DESHAR: The Truth.

(DESHAR smiles.)

DENG: Yes, the clear, objective, truth. *(Pause.)* Ask.

DESHAR: The Blacksmith comes to the Buddha while he is on his death bed. He asks the Buddha to bring his dead child to life and says if you are enlightened, bring my child back to life.

The Buddha realizes that the imposter is now, truly a blacksmith and asks him to sit next to his bed. The Buddha has two seeds in his fist. One which can bring the child back to her recent life and give her the suffering of death all over again. Another which makes the Blacksmith realize, that there is no magic in the first seed, and the child in fact lives on in the other children in the kingdom. Which seed should the Blacksmith take?

DENG: This isn't a polygraph question.

DESHAR: But this is the only question.

DENG: Liu… *(Looks at her picture and cries.)*

DESHAR: Deng… My voice has been heard. Relieve me.

(Pause.)

DENG: Ask.

DESHAR: If you could save your child from suffering with a lie that would take her life, would you lie, inspector Deng?

(DENG looks at her. Silence.)

DESHAR: If you could save your child from suffering with a lie that would take her life, would you lie, inspector Deng?

DENG: The Truth is, yes. I would lie. I would lie.

(The beeps come on, the red light switches on.)

(Silence.)

DESHAR: Relieve me, Inspector Deng. The truth has been recorded.

(DENG falls on the floor in exhaustion, next to GAPHEL.)

(Takes out his gun and points to DESHAR.)

(Gun Shot.)

(Blackout.)

Epilogue

JIA is in a big field full of objects of little girls. Her daughter who is lying down gets up. Smiles and walks up to her. Sounds of children playing in a playground.

JIA: Liu. *(Smiles.)*

LIU: I knew you would come Mama.

JIA: Here's your diary Liu. I found it.

LIU: Where's...

JIA: He couldn't make it, my child. He is at the prison.

LIU: While I was running from the mob, they threw petrol on me Mama. Look here... *(Her entire back is burnt.)*

(JIA runs to her. Liu stops her.)

LIU: Don't touch me Mama. My skin will come off. It won't look good on you.

JIA: You're alive aren't you?

LIU: Is he alive Mama?

JIA: Who?

LIU: His Holiness. *(Smiles.)*

JIA: Yes he is.

LIU: They said he will live till 120 Mama. He can choose his time of death.

JIA: Are you alive my dear?

LIU: If he can chose his time of death, why didn't he save me Mama?

JIA: He is a god in exile, my dear. A Supreme being of the homeless. He has a lot on his plate.

LIU: Look here Mama…this is Tenzin, and that is Tashi. They were in such a rush Mama…they even burnt Tibetan children Mama? Will you tell their Pah-la that they are dead mama? Their god couldn't save them too.

JIA: You are alive aren't you my child?

LIU: No Mama. You got my diary. They got me.

JIA: Did it hurt Liu?

LIU: No mama. Before I burnt they stabbed me in the back.

JIA: Good. It didn't hurt.

LIU: No mama. They were compassionate.

JIA: This is the end Liu.

(Pause.)

LIU: May I ask you something, Mama?

JIA: Yes, Liu.

LIU: Why does god always appear as a man, Mama?

JIA:

LIU: Always? Everywhere?

JIA:

JIA: May I ask you something, Liu?

LIU: Yes Mama.

JIA: Do you feel like revenge?

LIU: No Mama.

JIA: Why?

LIU: When we die, we turn non violent. *(Laughs.)*

JIA: Really?

LIU: The dead can't die anymore Mama. Life is an act of violence.

JIA: And now. Is there afterlife? Or reincarnation?

LIU: No Mama. Nothing.

JIA: Then?

LIU: Then nothing. There is nothing Mama. There really is nothing to die for.

JIA: Are you disappointed, my dear?

LIU: No Mama. It feels free. *(Pause.)*

LIU: May I ask you something, mama?

JIA: Yes my dear.

LIU: Are you alive Mama? *(Pause.)*

JIA: Yes. I feel hatred.

I am alive. I am alive, my child.

To live is to hate.

END OF PLAY.